Don't Stop The COOK!

A Complete Guide to Caribbean Food Recipes

Over 300 Delicious Food Recipes
from the Florida Keys and all of the
Caribbean Islands

~ by Pro Publishing ~

~Special Thanks~

Many thanks to everybody who had input in making this book.
To compile all the recipes and to put the book together was a lot
of fun, and at times also frustrating.

Don't Stop The COOK!

Published by Pro Publishing, Inc.
www.BlueWaterIslands.com
SW Ranches, FL 33331, Florida
© 2004 by Pro Publishing, Inc.

Printed and Designed by www.PostCardusa.com
PCUSA2961

Printed in Korea

~Table of Contents~

Introduction 4
Conversion Charts 10
Breads 11
Sauces & Seasonings 17
Appetizers 23
Soups 33
Salads 41
Side Dishes 49
Seafood 57
Meat 77
Poultry 89
Desserts 97
Ingredients Glossary 118
Index 122

Caribbean Cuisine

The Caribbean Islands are a chain of more than 7,000 islands, measuring 2,500 miles from the coast of Florida to Venezuela. The largest islands known as the West Indies are: Cuba, Jamaica, Puerto Rico and Hispaniola, which represents the Dominican Republic and Haiti.

Caribbean cooking is a combination of the cuisine from all the islands. Many distinct cultures have influenced and are associated with Caribbean cuisine. The oldest known is the Amerindians, which consists of the Carib and Arawak tribes from South America. They lived on these islands when Christopher Columbus arrived in America. The Amerindians farmed cassava, corn, sweet potatoes, garlic, tobacco and many varieties of peppers. European influences came from the Spanish in Cuba, Dominican Republic and Puerto Rico; the French in Haiti, St. Martin, Guadeloupe, St. Barths and Martinique; the British in the British Virgin Islands, Jamaica, Barbados, Grenada; and the Dutch in St. Maarten, Aruba and Curaçao. African slaves introduced pigeon peas, beans, yams, okra, ackee and taro. Also the indentured servants from India and China brought their original foods and cooking methods to these islands. The East Indians introduced yogurt, curries, spices, and ghee (clarified butter). The Chinese contributed rice, oranges and their own cultural cooking methods.

Some islands have spicier foods than others. Cuba, the Dominican Republic and Puerto Rico cook with mild bell peppers, while the rest of the Caribbean uses fiery peppers. In the Virgin Islands, Scotch Bonnet, Congo or Habanero peppers are widely used and are considered to be some of the hottest condiments in the world!

The combination of rice and beans is very popular throughout the Caribbean. In Cuba, black beans are served on top of rice. The beans in Jamaica are red, and the mixture is flavored with coconut milk. On some other islands, the rice and beans combination is seasoned with sweet peppers and tomatoes, bacon or hot peppers. Djon djon is rice and a type of lima bean from Haiti that is cooked in broth with dark mushrooms from the Haitian highlands. In the British Virgin Islands, rice is combined with pigeon peas, a yellow pea-like seed that originally came from Africa.

Caribbean cuisine today has the influences of a diverse group of people. It is flavored with aromatic seasonings, tropical fruits, a vast variety of delectable seafood, exotic prepared meats and poultry dishes.

Pirates, Buccaneers, and Privateers

Piracy is the crime of robbery or an act of violence for private gain on the high sea. It is committed by the captain and/or their crew outside the normal jurisdiction of any nation or without any authority from any government. The people who engage in these acts are called "Pirates". Legislation and treaties between countries have sometimes applied the term "piracy" in order to attack high sea ships legally and with authorization by a government. Such acts, however, were not regarded as piracy under the law of nations. Those were called "privateering", as it was acting for a political purpose. This was officially abolished by the Declaration of Paris in 1856. The United States and other nations did not follow this declaration.

Piracy has existed for a long time. Phoenicians combined piracy with their usual seafaring business. European coastlines were terrorized by the Vikings from the 9th through the 11th century. A Hanseatic group was formed in the 13th century to create a mutual defense against pirates roaming the North and Baltic Seas. In the Mediterranean Sea, Muslim ships scoured for loot and slaves. Then, in the 17th century, Algerian pirates operated out of northern Africa all the way up the English Channel. Algiers was the pirates stronghold into the mid 19th century.

The laws, in terms of piracy, have been revised and extended to include crimes such as slave trading. Every independent state has the power and can regulate its own criminal laws to declare offenses to be piracy that usually are not considered such by international laws. These local laws can only be enforced in the jurisdiction that created them. Similar regulations and laws may be adopted by other states without a special agreement between those states. The officers of one state may not arrest or punish pirates for offenses committed outside their jurisdiction.

"**Buccaneer**" was an official title for English, Dutch, and French seafarers of the 17th century. Daring seamen such as Englishmen Sir Francis Drake and Sir Richard Hawkins became wealthy in operations against Spain. Those men were lured by the riches of the merchant ships mostly in the Caribbean Sea and off the coast of North America. They harassed Spanish ships and colonies in the New World, mainly during the second half of the 17th century.

The most famous buccaneer, Sir Henry Morgan, was born in England. Privateers and buccaneers were different. They had official government commissions. Buccaneers rarely had such a commission. Also, pirates attacked ships of all nations, privateers only what the government decided.

The name "buccaneer" came from the practice of raiding Hispanola and stealing cattle from the plantations. They dried the meat on grills in a process called "boucan" by the French, and then sold to vessels. Later, the buccaneers used Jamaica as a base operation. With their leader, Captain Morgan, they captured Panama in 1671. The era came to an end in the early 18th century. Buccaneers were then hired by their governments to fight privateers in the War of the Spanish Succession between 1701 and 1714.

"**Privateer**" is the term applied to a privately owned ship with a commission of a hostile nation to initiate naval warfare. It is called "marque." Privateering is different from piracy which is carried out without the consent of a government. It was abolished by the "Declaration of Paris" in 1856, but the United States did not support it. Under the U.S. Constitution, Congress had the power to issue "letters of marque." It was carried out during the American Revolution and the War of 1812.

Fifteen men on a dead man's chest
    Yo, ho, ho, and a bottle of rum
Drink and the devil had done for the rest
    Yo, ho, ho, and a bottle of rum.
        -Robert Louis Stevenson, *Treasure Island* 1883

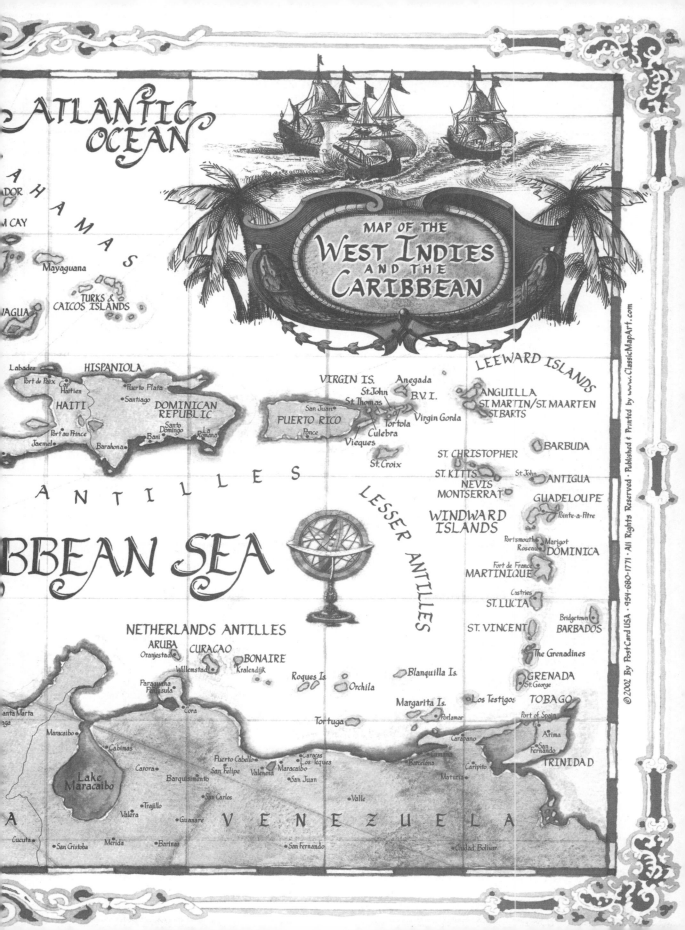

MAP OF THE WEST INDIES AND THE CARIBBEAN

ATLANTIC OCEAN

BAHAMAS

...DOR

...M CAY

Mayaguana

...AGUA

TURKS & CAICOS ISLANDS

LEEWARD ISLANDS

Labadee
HISPANIOLA
Port de Paix
Cap Haitien
Puerto Plata
Santiago
HAITI
DOMINICAN REPUBLIC
Port au Prince
Santo Domingo
La Romana
Jaemel
Barahona
Bani

VIRGIN IS.
Anegada
St. John
B.V.I.
St. Thomas
San Juan
PUERTO RICO
Tortola
Virgin Gorda
Ponce
Culebra
Vieques
St. Croix

ANGUILLA
ST. MARTIN/ST. MAARTEN
ST. BARTS

BARBUDA

ST. CHRISTOPHER
St. John
ST. KITTS
ANTIGUA
NEVIS
MONTSERRAT
GUADELOUPE
Pointe-a-Pitre

A N T I L L E S

CARIBBEAN SEA

LESSER ANTILLES

WINDWARD ISLANDS

Portsmouth
Marigot
Roseau
DOMINICA

Fort de France
MARTINIQUE

Castries
ST. LUCIA

Bridgetown
ST. VINCENT
BARBADOS

The Grenadines

GRENADA
St. George

TOBAGO

NETHERLANDS ANTILLES

ARUBA
CURACAO
Oranjestad
BONAIRE
Willemstad
Kralendijk

Roques Is.
Orchila
Blanquilla Is.

Margarita Is.
Los Testigos
Porlamar

Paraguana Peninsula
Cora

Tortuga

Port of Spain
Carapano
Arima
San Fernando
TRINIDAD

anta Marta
...ga
Maracaibo
Cabimas
Carora
Puerto Cabello
Caracas
Los Teques
Sumana
Barcelona
San Felipe
Maracaibo
Caripito
Valencia
San Juan
Maturia
Barquisimento
Lake Maracaibo
San Carlos
Valle
Trajillo
Valera
Guanare
V E N E Z U E L A
Cucuta
San Cristoba
Merida
Barinas
San Fernando
Ciudad Bolivar

~Measurement Conversions~

Measurement	Standard Equivalent	Metric Equivalent
Dash	less than 1/8 teaspoon	————
1 teaspoon	60 drops	5 ml
1 Tablespoon	3 teaspoons	15 ml
2 Tablespoons	1 fluid ounce	30 ml
4 Tablespoons	¼ cup	60 ml
5⅓ Tablespoons	⅓ cup	80 ml
6 Tablespoons	⅜ cup	90 ml
8 Tablespoons	½ cup	120 ml
10⅔ Tablespoons	⅔ cup	160 ml
12 Tablespoons	¾ cup	180 ml
16 Tablespoons	1 cup (8 fluid ounces)	240 ml
1 cup	½ pint (8 fluid ounces)	240 ml
2 cups	1 pint	480 ml
1 pint	16 ounces	480 ml (0.473 liter)
1 quart	2 pints	960 ml (0.95 liter)
2.1 pints	1.05 quarts (0.26 gallon)	1 liter
2 quarts	½ gallon	————
4 quarts	1 gallon	3.8 liters

~Weight Conversions~

Weight	Standard Equivalent	Metric Equivalent
1 ounce	16 drams	28 grams
1 pound	16 ounces	454 grams
1 pound	2 cups liquid	————
2.20 pounds	————	1 kilogram

~Temperature Conversions~

Fahrenheit	300	325	350	375	400	425	475
Celsius	149	163	176	191	205	218	246

Breads

Banana Breakfast Bread
~ Bahamas ~

4 bananas, overripe
¼ teaspoon ground cinnamon
½ cup butter
½ cup raisins

2½ cups all-purpose flour
¼ teaspoon ground nutmeg
2 eggs, beaten
½ cup nuts, crushed

2½ teaspoons baking powder
½ teaspoon vanilla extract
⅓ cup sugar
dash salt

Preheat oven to 350°F. Sift all dry ingredients. Peel and mash bananas well with a fork. Add vanilla. Cream the butter and sugar in a mixing bowl. Add eggs. Add the banana and flour mixtures slowly. Mix until smooth. Add raisins and finely chopped nuts. Pour batter into greased loaf pan. Bake for 1 hour or until a knife is inserted in the middle and comes out slightly moist. Cool for 15 minutes, and turn over onto a wire cooling rack. Makes 1 loaf.

Banana-Vanilla Muffins
~ St. Thomas ~

1¼ cups mashed bananas
½ cup butter
1½ cups flour

1 egg, beaten
½ teaspoon vanilla

¾ cup granulated sugar
1 teaspoon baking soda

Preheat oven to 350°F. Combine bananas, egg, sugar, butter and vanilla. Dissolve baking soda in 1 tablespoon of hot water and add to mixture. Mix until creamy. Add the flour and lightly mix. Bake for 20 minutes or until golden brown and when an inserted toothpick comes out clean.

Coconut Bread
~ Jamaica ~

4 cups all-purpose flour
¼ teaspoon cinnamon
2 tablespoons whole raisins
½ cup evaporated milk

3½ teaspoons baking powder
dash of salt
2¾ cups shredded coconut
½ cup sweet butter, melted

½ teaspoon nutmeg
2 cups brown sugar
2 eggs, well beaten
1 tablespoon water

Preheat oven to 325°F. Butter and lightly flour 2 (9x5 inch) bread pans. Sift dry ingredients together into a mixing bowl. Stir in fruits. Add blended eggs, milk and melted butter. Bake for approximately 1 hour, making sure center dough tests dry with a wooden toothpick. Cook on baking shelf. Makes 2 loaves.

Coconut Rolls
~ Granada ~

Pastry: 2 pounds white flour   1 cup sugar   milk, for desired consistency
¾-1 cup melted butter   2 teaspoons baking powder

Fruit filling: 2 cups coconut, grated   2 cups strawberry, guava or sorrel jam   ¼ cup ground cinnamon
2 tablespoons vanilla extract

Preheat oven to 300ºF. Mix together all of the fruit filling ingredients and set aside. For the pastry, blend sugar and flour. Add in melted butter and pour the milk in slowly until dough is desired consistency. Set aside for 1 hour. Separate into 4 pastry portions. With each one, roll out to a thin dough base, making sure to flour the surface before rolling out. Brush surface with a coating of milk and spread fruit filling evenly onto pastry. Roll the fruit filling and dough into a tube. Bake on a greased and floured pan until golden color. May top with a dust of cinnamon and/or sugar, if desired. Cut at an angle into 4 inch slices.

Caribbean French Rum Toast
~ Martinique ~

Syrup: 1 cup gold rum   2 cups maple syrup   4 tablespoons coconut cream
½ teaspoon nutmeg

Toast: 8 slices slightly stale bread   4 eggs   ½ cup milk
½ cup rum   ½ teaspoon cinnamon   ½ teaspoon vanilla
2 tablespoons butter

In a small saucepan at medium heat, combine rum, maple syrup, cream of coconut and nutmeg. Whisk together in a shallow bowl the eggs, milk, rum, cinnamon, vanilla and butter. Dip both sides of bread into the mixture and allow to soak for 30 seconds. In a skillet, add butter and cook each side of the bread until golden. Serve with butter and syrup. Serves 4.

Holiday Mango-Nut Bread
~ Islamorada, Florida Keys ~

1 ripe banana   2 eggs   4 ounces honey
¼ cup almonds, sliced   ½ cup butter, room temperature   ¾ cup light brown sugar
2 cups unbleached all-purpose flour   1 teaspoon baking soda   1 Key lime, juiced
¼ teaspoon salt   ¼ cup macadamia nuts   ¼ cup chopped pecans
1 cup ripe mango, peeled and cut into small cubes

Preheat oven to 375ºF. In a mixing bowl, mash banana and add rest of ingredients. Stir well. Pour into two loaf pans that are lightly greased. Bake until golden brown and a toothpick inserted in the middle comes out clean. Makes 2 loaves.

Johnny Cakes
~ Jamaica ~

4 cups all-purpose flour
1 teaspoon baking powder

dash of salt
4 cups vegetable oil, for frying

1 tablespoon butter
1½ cups water

Sift together dry ingredients. Blend in melted butter and water to create firm dough. Knead well. Dust a working surface with flour. Cut dough into 14 pieces and shape into a circle ½ inch thick. Heat oil until hot. Test by dropping a pinch of dough into oil, if it rises to the top, oil is ready. Fry a few cakes at a time to golden brown on each side. Drain and serve. Makes 14.

Pan Bati
~ Aruba ~

1 can evaporated milk
4 cups flour
1 cup water

2 cups cornmeal
2 tablespoons sugar

dash salt
2 tablespoons baking powder

In a large bowl, mix all ingredients together, adding enough water to make the mixture the consistency of pancake batter. Refrigerate overnight. Heat up griddle and pour on a small amount of olive oil. Pour mixture on hot griddle, when brown turn over. The mixture should be about 16 inches in diameter. While on griddle, beat the bread on both sides with a flat knife. Cut pieces into triangles and serve with meal. Serves 12.

Pan de Naranja
~ El Coche ~

¾ cup mixed nuts
4½ cups flour
1 tablespoon orange rind, grated
1 cup orange marmalade

1 orange bread
2 eggs, beaten
1½ teaspoon salt

1½ cups milk
4 teaspoons baking powder
¼ cup sugar

Preheat oven to 350°F. Sift salt, baking powder and flour together. In a separate bowl, mix sugar, marmalade and orange rind together, then add flour mixture. Gradually add milk and eggs. Add some flour to nuts and then shake off. Add to dough mixture and fold in. On a greased and floured baking pan, place bread and allow to set for 10 minutes. Bake for 35 minutes or until a knife inserted in center comes out clean. Serves 4.

Pineapple Bread
~ Antigua ~

2 cups fresh crushed pineapple
1 egg
1 teaspoon salt

⅔ cup light brown sugar
2 cups unbleached all-purpose flour

⅓ cup butter
4 teaspoons baking powder

Preheat oven to 350°F. Grease a 9 inch cake pan. Cream the butter in a large bowl and slowly add sugar, beating well. Place mixture in pan and bake for 1 hour, or until light brown. Serve warm. Makes 1 loaf.

Pineapple-Banana Rum Bread
~ Jamaica ~

½ cup white rum
4 tablespoons butter
⅓ cup yogurt, plain
½ tablespoon baking powder
1 teaspoon cinnamon, ground

½ cup dehydrated pineapple, diced
1 extra large egg
2 cups all-purpose flour
1 teaspoon nutmeg, ground
dash salt

¾ cup sugar
2 very ripe bananas, mashed
½ tablespoon baking soda
1 teaspoon allspice, ground
½ cup pecans, chopped

Prepare oven at 350°F. Soak pineapple in rum for 1 hour in a small container. Beat sugar and butter together into a mixing bowl, while adding in the egg, until light and fluffy. Blend in mashed banana. Then add in yogurt, this may create a separated texture which is fine. Sift together dry ingredients in another bowl. Add sifted ingredients into the banana mixture and blend well. Drain soaked pineapple and spoon into the batter along with the chopped pecans. Pour batter into loaf a 9 inch loaf pan and bake for about 55 minutes. Cool for 10 minutes before turning out. Makes 1 loaf.

Port Royal Bammie
~ Jamaica ~

2 pounds sweet cassava

Peel and grate sweet cassava in a food processor. Place the grated cassava in a piece of cheesecloth and squeeze out the juice letting the moist cassava flour remain. Place in a bowl and rub eliminating any lumps. Place large skillet on low flame. When skillet is hot, add in cassava flour to make a flat cake about 6 inches in diameter, ¾ inch thick. Cook until cassava sets. Turn over and repeat on other side. Remove from pan and scrape to remove any scorched parts. For added flavor, a drop of milk may be added and baked in a hot oven, browned under a grill, or fried with bacon fat.
Makes 1 cake.

Puerto Plata Sweet Corn Bread
~ Dominican Republic ~

¾ cup yellow cornmeal
½ cup flour
½ teaspoon nutmeg, grated
3 tablespoons dark brown sugar
¼ cup fresh or unsweetened canned coconut milk

¼ cup dark raisins
½ cup milk
¼ cup coconut, grated
3 teaspoons baking powder

1 egg
¼ teaspoon salt
3 tablespoons coconut oil
½ teaspoon ground cinnamon

Preheat oven to 425°F. Grease a 6 inch square baking pan. In a large bowl, add all ingredients and combine until mixture is a smooth thick batter. Pour the batter into the prepared pan and bake for 20 minutes until light brown. Serve hot with butter. Makes 1 dozen.

Roti
~ Guyana ~

2 cups unbleached white flour
water, to add to dough

¼ teaspoon baking powder
¼ teaspoon salt

corn oil, for grilling

In a large bowl, sift all dry ingredients and add enough water to make a stiff dough. Form the dough into 4-6 balls and flatten each ball with a rolling pin. Spread each roti with corn oil and a little bit of flour. Fold roti back into balls by turning the ends in on each other let them stand for 30 minutes. Heat a griddle and roll roti into flat crepe like forms. Cook until light brown, turning constantly for 3 minutes. To keep from sticking, pour a small amount of corn oil on top and turn over. Remove roti and place in the palm of your hand and clap 3 times taking care not to burn yourself. Serve with chicken curry or chutney. Makes 4-6 rotis.

Star Fruit Wake-Me-Ups
~ Florida Keys ~

3 star fruits, sliced ¼ inch thick
dash salt
2 tablespoons butter, melted
maple syrup, to taste

¾ cup cornmeal
2 extra large eggs, separated
1 tablespoon sugar
6 tablespoons all-purpose flour

1 tablespoon baking powder
1 cup milk
½ teaspoon cream of tartar

Sift together flour, cornmeal, baking powder and salt into bowl. In a separate bowl, beat egg yolks, milk and melted butter. Add to sifted ingredients and stir together. Whisk egg whites, sugar, and cream of tartar until firm in a separate bowl. Slowly add to cornmeal mix and blend into a batter. Set aside. Heat oil to moderate high on a griddle surface. Layer a star fruit slice onto pan and follow with the batter poured over the fruit, about 2 tablespoons for each pancake. When beginning to bubble, flip over and cook golden brown other side, about 1 minute. Place on a dish, cover while cooking the rest of the pancakes. For presentation, decorate with slices of star fruit. This dish can be repeated with other delicious tropical fruits. Makes 24 cakes.

Sauces & Seasonings

Adobo Powder
~ Puerto Rico ~

1 tablespoon oregano, dried
dash salt

1 tablespoon onion powder
freshly ground pepper

1 tablespoon garlic powder

Combine seasoning mixture and place in a covered jar. An excellent meat seasoning and a staple for specialty island dishes.

Carib Cool Papaya-Mango Sauce
~ St. Kitts ~

1 papaya, peeled, seeded and diced
1 mango, peeled, pitted and diced
¼ cup dry white vinegar
¼ cup raisins
2 tablespoons Dijon-style mustard
1 teaspoon red hot sauce
2 tablespoons Worcestershire sauce

½ cup red onion, diced
1 teaspoon island seasoning
3 cloves garlic, minced
2 teaspoons ginger, minced
2 tablespoons brown sugar
½ teaspoon ground allspice

1 tomato, diced
1 cup red wine vinegar
¼ cup brown sugar
2 Scotch Bonnet Peppers
¼ teaspoon white pepper
¼ teaspoon salt

In a non reactive saucepan, add all ingredients and cook on low heat, stirring constantly. Simmer for 15 minutes until mixture has a jam-like consistency. Allow to cool at room temperature. Add mixture to food processor and process for 20 seconds until sauce is smooth with only a few chunks. Serve or refrigerate. If refrigerated the sauce should keep for 2-3 weeks. Makes 2 cups.

Cassareep
~ Guyana ~

4 pounds sweet cassava, peeled
1 tablespoon dark brown sugar

1 cup cool water
½ teaspoon ground cloves

¾ teaspoon cinnamon

Mince cassava. Put in blender with water and purée. Let set for 5 minutes. Place purée into moist cheesecloth and strain out liquid by twisting and squeezing cassava so liquid passes through into a bowl. Discard flesh and pour juice, with other ingredients, into a pan. Bring to a boil and simmer, stirring occasionally until the mixture thickens. Pour into a sterilized container and refrigerate. Makes 1 cup.

Coconut Cream
~ Puerto Rico ~

1½ to 2 pound coconut

2 cups water

Prepare fresh coconut milk. Set aside until a thick cream rises to the surface. Scoop off and use as a cream. Store remaining milk for other recipes. Makes ¾ cup.

Coquimol
~ Haiti ~

¾ pint coconut cream
¾ cup water
1½ teaspoons white rum

6 ounces sugar
½ teaspoon vanilla essence

6 egg yolks
dash nutmeg

Boil water and sugar over medium heat, stirring occasionally. Increase heat and cook until sugar and water form syrup. Test by dropping a small amount into cold water, a soft ball should form if ready. Remove from heat and slowly stir in the coconut cream. In a separate bowl, beat the egg yolks, stir in coconut mixture and 3 tablespoons of the syrup. Slowly stir the egg mixture into saucepan. Return to heat until sauce has the consistency of double cream. Add vanilla and rum. Pour into a closable jar when slightly cooled. Sprinkle with nutmeg, seal and refrigerate until fully cooled. Serve over Gâteau de Patate (see page: 106). Serves 6.

Fruity Marmalade
~ Montserrat ~

½ grapefruit, sliced and seeded, leaving rind on
2 fresh oranges, sliced and seeded, leaving rind on
½ pineapple, peeled and sliced   ½ teaspoon ground nutmeg

8 cups water
5 cups sugar
1 lime, juiced

Layer alternately pineapple, grapefruit and orange slices into medium saucepan. Top with water and bring to a boil. Reduce heat to medium and cook for around 25 minutes until rind is soft. Cool and remove pith. Set aside overnight. In the morning, pour off liquid and reserve. Mince rind and add to fruit. Mix sugar, lime juice, nutmeg, and 1½ cups of fruit liquid. Add to fruit batch and cook uncovered. Allow to thicken, occasionally stirring. Cook about 50-60 minutes. Place into sterilized jars. Makes 2 pounds.

Guava Jelly
~ St.Vincent ~

10 under ripe guavas   1 cup sugar   1 cup lime juice

Wash and peel guavas and cut in half. Place in saucepan and cover with water. Bring to a boil and cook for 10 minutes until soft. Strain through a colander and then through a fine sieve. Do not rub through sieve. Reserve water. In a medium pot, heat lime juice. Slowly add sugar and let dissolve before mixture boils. For every cup of liquid add 1 teaspoon of lime juice. Boil briskly removing the gum that appears with a wooden spoon until mixture gels in the pan. Test by dipping fork into mixture. When mixture is firm, it is ready. Pour in warm sterilized jars. Seal and store.

Key Lime Relish
~ Florida Keys ~

¼ cup pineapple, crushed
2 tablespoons green pepper, minced
1 tablespoon light brown sugar
¼ teaspoon dry mustard

½ cup sour cream
1 tablespoon onion, minced
1½ teaspoons Key lime peel, grated
pinch of cloves, ground

2 tablespoons Key lime, diced
¼ teaspoon celery salt

Mix all ingredients together and chill in refrigerator. Makes 1 cup.

Mango Chutney
~ Guyana ~

12 unripe mangoes, peeled
2 tablespoons vegetable oil
1 tablespoon masala (see below)

10 garlic cloves
4 teaspoons cumin
dash salt

4 large hot red peppers
2 tablespoons garam masala
2 tablespoons mustard oil

In a large bowl, grate mangoes. Finely chop garlic and hot peppers and toss together with grated mango. Heat up oil in a pan and simmer all ingredients together for 5 minutes, except the mustard oil. Let cool. Fill sterilized storage jars and top with mustard oil and seal. As the chutney is consumed, add mustard oil as needed for preservation. Properly preserved, the chutney may be enjoyed for months. Makes 21 ounces.

Mango Mojo
~ Key West, Florida Keys ~

1 large ripe mango, peeled and cut from the pit, then into ¼ inch slices
¼ cup fresh squeezed Key lime juice   1 tablespoon ground cumin
1 large onion, cut into ¼ inch slices   1 cup dry white wine
2 cups fresh squeezed orange juice   1 teaspoon freshly ground black pepper

3 tablespoons virgin olive oil
1 teaspoon dry oregano
2 cloves garlic, minced
1 tablespoon salt

Cook onion for about 5 minutes in a saucepan over medium heat until soft. Add garlic and sauté for 1 minute. Add oregano, cumin, salt and pepper, and sauté an additional 2 minutes. Add orange juice, white wine, Key lime juice and mango. Simmer mixture for 15 minutes. Cool for 10 minutes and transfer to a blender, purée until smooth. The mojo is ready to use. To store, pour into hot sterilized jars and seal airtight. The mojo will keep for 2-3 weeks. Makes 4 cups.

Masala
~ Guyana ~

2 tablespoons black cumin seeds
3 whole cloves

2 tablespoons mustard seeds
½ teaspoon pumpkin spice

2 tablespoons fenugreek seeds

Toast seeds separately by roasting in a dry frying pan. Stir until evenly roasted, about 3 minutes. Grind seeds and cloves with a mortar. Add pumpkin spice. Store in an airtight jar. Great with Mango Chutney (see above). Makes 6 tablespoons.

Mazola
~ Jamaica ~

2 tablespoons toasted mustard seeds
2 cloves, whole
2 tablespoons toasted fenugreek seeds

2 tablespoons black cumin seeds, toasted
½ teaspoon cinnamon, mixed spice, or pumpkin pie spice

Toast the seeds separately by placing in a moderatly heated pan in an even layer. Gently roll with a flat spatula until they are darkened, about 3-4 minutes. Grind the seeds together, including the cloves, with a mortar and pestle or small nut grinder. Stir in cinnamon or similar spice. Place in an airtight storage jar. Unlimited shelf life. Makes 6 tablespoons.

Mojo Criollo
~ Cuba ~

10 garlic cloves, peeled
1 teaspoon salt

1 cup cooking vegetable oil

1 cup sour orange juice

Combine garlic, salt and orange juice. Heat oil and whisk all ingredients. Pour over meat.

Montego Bay Pineapple Chutney
~ Jamaica ~

3 cups fresh pineapple, crushed
1 thumb-size piece ginger, scraped and minced
1 cup cane vinegar

1 cup dark brown sugar

1 medium onion, chopped
1 Scotch Bonnet Chile

In a blender, add ginger, onion, pineapple, chile and a little vinegar to moisten mixture. Pour mixture in a non reactive saucepan and add sugar and vinegar. Stir well making sure there are no clumps of chile. Place saucepan over medium heat and bring to a boil. Stir constantly to avoid sticking. Reduce heat and cook for 25 minutes until it thickens. Pour chutney into scalded glass jars. Keep refrigerated. Will keep in refrigerator for 3 weeks. Makes 2 cups.

Pepper and Caraili Sauce
~ St. Vincent ~

12 hot red peppers, seeded
1 leaf Shadow Bennie
3 sprigs chives
1 tablespoon lime juice
dash salt

3 caraili, minced
1 carrot, peeled and sliced
4 garlic cloves
2 cups vegetable oil

2 onions, minced
1 bunch parsley
½ cup vinegar
1 teaspoon sugar

Cut the peppers into thin slices. In a little salted water, bring caraili to a boil. Remove from heat, cut lengthwise and remove seeds. Slice thinly. Combine ingredients and simmer for 5 minutes. Let cool. Bottle and cover tightly.

Pirated Thyme-Mustard Sauce
~ Caribbean ~

3 tablespoons fresh thyme leaves
⅛ teaspoon white pepper

¼ cup Dijon-style mustard

¾ cup heavy cream

In a small bowl, combine all ingredients. Before serving, warm the mustard sauce in microwave until it is hot. Serve with Treasured Chicken (see page: 96).

Sofrito
~ Antigua ~

1 tablespoon olive oil
2 garlic cloves, crushed
2 tomatoes, seeded and chopped
2 tablespoons of annatto oil (made from oil and annatto seeds)

2 ounces ham, minced
1 onion, minced
1 teaspoon fresh oregano, diced

1 ounce bacon, minced
1 teaspoon parsley, chopped
½ bell pepper, chopped

Brown minced ham and bacon in a pan with oil over a moderate high heat. Add in garlic and onion. On a low heat, place in the remainder of the ingredients, except for the annatto oil. Simmer for about 10 minutes. Then add oil, and raise heat to medium, cooking for an additional minute. Makes 3 cups.

Sorrel Jam
~ Antigua ~

2 pounds sorrel sepals, seeded
1 cup water

3 pounds white sugar

1 stick of cinnamon

Wash sorrel sepals well. In a large pot, put water, cinnamon and sepals. Boil until sepals soften and remove from heat. Add in the sugar. Pour into blender and mix until smooth. Return to heat and boil until mixture sets. Remove and allow mixture to cool down. Pour mixture into a canning jar and seal. Keep jam refrigerated. To make jelly, follow the above recipe. Instead, add enough water to cover the sepals and boil. Do not crush the sepals or strain water. Add 1 cup of sugar for each cup of juice. Boil until set. Remove any scum from the surface. Pour into canning jars.

Virgin Seasoning
~ St. John ~

6 peppers, sweet
5 sprigs chives, minced
1 teaspoon fresh thyme
¼ teaspoon allspice
dash mace

½ hot pepper, seeded and minced
1 celery stalk, minced
1 teaspoon freshly ground black pepper
dash nutmeg
dash ground clove

6 garlic cloves, crushed
1 sprig parsley, diced
¼ cup salt
dash cinnamon

Grind all spices together and store in covered jar. This spice mixture is used with fish, poultry and meat, primarily as an exotic stuffing and flavor enhancer.

Appetizers

Acras de Morue
~ Guadeloupe ~

½ pound codfish, salted
1 scallion, including green top
½ Scotch Bonnet Pepper

2 sprigs fresh flat-leaf parsley
2 chives
vegetable oil, for frying

1 sprig fresh thyme
¼ teaspoon allspice

Acras Batter: 2 eggs
salt and freshly ground pepper

1 cup all-purpose flour

⅓ cup milk

Flake codfish. Grind to a thick paste in a food processor: codfish, parsley, thyme, chives, scallions, allspice, and chile. Fold the paste into the acras batter.

Acras Batter: Sift together flour and seasoning into a bowl. Hollow a "well" into the center of the seasoned flour. Break the eggs into the well one at a time while whisking the mixture. Slowly add in milk while whisking. Beat until batter becomes a thick paste. Cover with a dampened cloth and allow to rest for several hours. Prepare a deep fryer with 2 inches of corn oil heated between 350°F to 375°F. Before frying, mix together spiced codfish paste and the formed acras batter. Using a teaspoon measure, drop acras into hot oil and fry on both sides until golden. Lift out with a slotted spoon and drain on paper towels before serving. Serves 6.

Bacalaitos de San Juan
~ Puerto Rico ~

½ pound codfish, rinsed and flaked
1 Scotch Bonnet Chile, minced
2 garlic cloves, minced

2 cups all-purpose flour
2 cups water
dash freshly ground pepper

½ teaspoon baking powder
vegetable oil, for frying
dash salt

Sift together dry ingredients. Mix in flaked codfish, chile, garlic, spices, and water and stir well. In a heavy frying pan, heat 2 inches of oil between 350°F to 375°F. Drop the bacalaitos by the teaspoonful into the oil, only a few at a time, and cook until golden brown. Drain on paper towels before serving. Makes 24.

Bermudan Avocado Cocktail
~ Bermuda ~

2 large avocados
2 tablespoons dark rum
3 tablespoons passion fruit juice, pulp, or lime juice

½ cup olive oil
1 teaspoon sesame seeds

2 garlic cloves, crushed
cocktail toothpicks

Blend all ingredients, except avocado, into a marinade. Cut avocados in half, lengthwise. Using a small melon ball scoop, cut out avocado flesh into cocktail sized balls and place into marinade. Chill for 4 hours. Drain and insert a decorative cocktail toothpick into each avocado ball. Arrange onto a plate with gourmet lettuce greens. The marinade can be mixed with ¼ cup of yogurt or fresh sour cream and utilized as a dressing or avocado dipping sauce. Makes 36 pieces.

Bitterbal (Meat Croquettes)
~ Aruba ~

3 tablespoons butter
1½ cups finely chopped, cooked meat (roast beef, ham, veal, chicken or shrimp)
½ teaspoon Worcestershire sauce
dash salt and freshly ground pepper

3 tablespoons flour
1 tablespoon parsley, minced
1 cup fine cracker crumbs

¾ cup stock
1 egg, beaten
2 tablespoons water
½ cup mustard

Make a thick sauce of butter, flour and stock. Add meat, parsley, Worcestershire sauce, salt and pepper. Chill mixture and form 1 inch balls. Roll balls in crumbs. Combine egg and water. Dip balls in egg and water and roll in crumbs again. Fry balls in hot fat until golden brown. Serve hot with mustard. Makes 2 dozen.

Bol Jul (Brule Johl)
~ Barbados ~

1 pound salt cod
½ red bell pepper, chopped finely
2 tablespoons fresh lime juice

2 medium onions, chopped finely
1 hot pepper, seeded, chopped finely
½ teaspoon dried thyme

2 ripe firm tomatoes
¼ cup virgin olive oil
freshly ground black pepper

Cover salt cod with water and soak overnight. Drain and rinse fish. Discard skin and bones and shred fish into very small flakes. In a large bowl, combine fish with remaining ingredients. Serve chilled with lettuce, avocado slices and crackers. Serves 4.

Carcó (Pickled Conch)
~ Bonaire ~

1 pound carcó

6 cups water

1 teaspoon salt

Marinade: 2 cups white vinegar
12 clavos, or cloves
½ cup chicken broth

3 garlic cloves, crushed
2 onions, sliced

1 teaspoon allspice
2 hot peppers, finely chopped

Clean and peel. With a wooden mallet pound conch well, until it is half its thickness. Bring water and salt to a boil in a saucepan. Cook conch for several minutes. Drain and cut into bite-size pieces. Marinate and refrigerate for 24 hours. Serve with saltine crackers. Serves 12.

Chicharrones
~ Puerto Rico ~

1 pound pork rind, trimmed

2 teaspoons salt

¼ cup vegetable oil

In a saucepan, soak pork rind in salted water for one hour. Cover and boil for 10 minutes. Chop into small ¼ inch by ½ inch pieces. Dust with salt and set aside for 10 minutes. Heat oil to a moderate heat in a frying pan. Fry salted pork rind for 10 minutes, covered. Continue cooking partly covered until crisp, bubbly and light golden brown. Drain on paper towels. Serves 4.

Conch Fritters
~ Key West ~

1 pound conch, cleaned, pounded and cut into ¼ inch pieces
12 ounces flour, sifted   ½ ounce baking powder   1 egg, beaten
2 onions, minced   2 celery stalks, minced   dash hot sauce
dash salt   dash freshly ground pepper   2 green bell peppers, minced
                                                                vegetable oil, for frying

Make a stiff batter with egg, flour, baking powder, seasonings and a little water. Mix additional ingredients and let batter rest for 15 minutes. Deep fry fritters in vegetable oil until golden. Makes 18 fritters.

Fantasy Fest Shrimp-Mango Cocktail
~ Key West, Florida Keys ~

12 jumbo shrimps, shelled, deveined, cooked and chilled

Salsa: 1 large ripe mango, peeled and cut from the pit   ½ cup diced cucumber
2 tablespoons crushed peanuts   ½ cup diced watermelon   1 teaspoon salt
2 tablespoons fresh Key lime juice   2 tablespoons chopped fresh cilantro   1 small red onion
1 tablespoon extra virgin olive oil ½ teaspoon fresh ground pepper

Shell and clean jumbo shrimp. Place shrimp in boiling water for 10-20 minutes. Make sure shrimp is thoroughly cooked before placing in refrigerator to chill.

Salsa: Cut and peel ripe mango in half. Slice the first half of the mango into ½ inch wedges. Next, in a medium bowl combine the second half of the mango (diced) with red onion, cucumber, watermelon, Key lime juice, olive oil, cilantro, salt and pepper. Mix well and place in refrigerator for 1-4 hours. Place salsa in four stemmed glasses. Place 3 shrimps on each glass rim. Garnish with mango wedges and ½ tablespoons peanuts. Serves 4.

Fish Fritters
~ Bahamas ~

8 ounces salt cod, soaked overnight   1 cup self-rising flour   1 onion, finely chopped
1 egg, beaten   1 tablespoon vegetable oil   ¾ cup milk
1 tablespoon butter, melted   1 fresh red chili, seeded, and finely chopped
vegetable oil, for frying   lemon wedges, to garnish   dash salt

In a bowl, sift flour and salt. Mix together in another bowl egg, milk and melted butter. Stir in flour. Mix well to form a smooth batter. Add a little more milk if batter is too dry. Drain and rinse salt cod. Place in large saucepan and cover with cold water. Bring to a boil. Reduce heat, cover and simmer for 20 minutes until tender. Drain and cool. Discard skin and bones. Flake meat. In skillet heat oil, add onion. Cook for 10 minutes. Allow to cool slightly. Mix fish, onion and chili into the batter. Heat ½ inch of oil in skillet. Drop spoonfuls of batter mixture into oil a few at a time. Fry for about 2 minutes on each side or until golden brown. Serve with lemon wedges. Serves 6.

Fried Cracked Conch
~ Florida Keys ~

4 conches   fresh lime juice (to cover conch meat)   hot pepper sauce to taste
2 beaten eggs   1 cup all-purpose flour   2 beaten eggs
breadcrumbs or crushed crackers   dash salt   dash freshly ground pepper

Remove conch meat from shell. Pound with a wooden mallet until meat is twice its original size. Marinate in lime juice and hot pepper sauce for 1 hour. Do not refrigerate. Cut conch meat into bite-sized chunks. Dip meat pieces in flour, next egg and then dredge in the breadcrumbs. Deep-fry in hot vegetable oil until golden brown. Drain on layered paper towel. Serve while hot. Makes 18 pieces.

Frituras de Ñame
~ Dominican Republic ~

1 pound yams or sweet potatoes, peeled and grated   ¼ cup vegetable oil
2 egg yolks   1 tablespoon parsley, minced   1½ teaspoons salt
1 tablespoon onion, grated   dash freshly ground black pepper
1 tablespoon butter, melted and cooled

In a deep bowl, add butter, salt, pepper, yams, parsley and onion and mix well. Add in egg yolk and beat with a large spoon until thick enough to come away from sides of bowl like a solid mass. Line a large shallow baking dish with paper towels and place in oven. Preheat oven to the lowest setting. Place olive oil in a skillet and heat. Drop a tablespoon of mixture into hot oil. Fry 4 minutes on each side until golden and crisp around edges. Drain by placing on a lined dish and keep warm. Makes 20 round cakes.

Gratin de Chayote Squash
~ Martinique ~

4 chayote squash
2 onions, diced
2 garlic cloves, crushed
1 tablespoon all-purpose flour
½ cup breadcrumbs

2 tablespoons extra virgin olive oil
butter
4 scallions, chopped
¼ cup milk

dash salt
dash freshly ground pepper
1 tablespoon parsley, chopped
1 cup grated parmesan cheese

Cut each chayote in half and remove center core. Place in saucepan and cover with salted water. Boil approximately 20-30 minutes, until soft. Gently spoon out flesh using care to leave a ¼ inch shell. Mash chayote well. Sauté onions, scallions, garlic and parsley to a golden brown. While stirring in flour, cook for 1 minute. To avoid clumps, add milk while stirring. Finally, stir in cheese. Blend in mashed chayote and half of the breadcrumbs. Preheat oven to 400°F oven. Fill the chayote shells with the blended mix and place on baking sheet. Sprinkle with breadcrumbs, cheese, and lightly pepper. Dab on butter. Bake for 10-15 minutes, until golden brown. Serve and enjoy. Serves 8.

Haitian Corn Fritters
~ Haiti ~

¼ chopped seeded hot pepper
1 onion, chopped
1 teaspoon parsley, chopped
1 beaten egg

10 ounces flour
½ sweet red pepper, chopped
1 teaspoon baking soda
dash salt

1 can sweet corn
1 garlic clove, chopped
1 cup milk
dash freshly ground pepper

In a blender, mix garlic, peppers and corn. Pour into a bowl and add baking powder, parsley, flour, salt and pepper. Mix well. Add egg and milk until the batter thickens. Add oil to frying pan, when hot spoon in batter. Fry until golden brown turning them occasionally. Remove drain with paper towel and serve.

Jamaican Patties
~ Jamaica ~

9 ounces ground lamb or beef
1 garlic clove, crushed
2 large tomatoes, peeled and chopped

1 tablespoon olive oil
1 hot pepper, minced
1-2 teaspoons curry powder

1 red onion, minced
1 beaten egg, for glazing
dash salt and ground pepper

Pastry: 3 cups white flour

1 teaspoon ground turmeric

¼ cup butter

Sauté onion and garlic in oil for 10 minutes in large skillet. Stir in beef or lamb until evenly browned. Add tomatoes, hot pepper, curry and seasoning. Simmer with an additional ¼ cup of water for about 15-20 minutes, until liquid evaporates. Set aside and allow to cool.

Pastry: Sift together dry ingredients. Roll in butter until there is a crumbled consistency. Pour in 3 tablespoons of water and make a firm dough. Cover and refrigerate for an hour. Prepare oven at 400°F. Portion the dough into 8 pieces. Roll out each one into a 7 inch circle. Drop a spoonful of meat filling onto half of the pastry. Dab water on edge of pastry, fold over filling and press to seal. Arrange in a flat baking pan. Brush tops with egg glaze. Bake until golden, about 30 minutes. Makes 8 patties.

Key Largo Key Lime Mango Shrimp
~ Key Largo, Florida Key ~

Dip: 1 cup of yogurt, flavored with Key lime
1 tablespoon lime juice   1 cup mango, puréed

Shrimp and Seasoned Batter: 1 pound shrimp, cleaned and prepared   milk
1 cup shredded sweet coconut   2 eggs, beaten   3 cups olive oil
1 cup breadcrumbs (panko-Japanese style recommended)

Blend together all the ingredients for the dip and chill in refrigerator. Soak prepared shrimp covered lightly with milk for 10-20 minutes. Toss together coconut and breadcrumbs and place on a flat preparation plate or pan. Dip shrimp into eggs and roll all surfaces on breading. Set aside on a plate ready for the next preparation step. Fry shrimp in hot oil until golden brown. Remove and drain on paper towel. Display shrimp on an attractive platter with dipping sauce. Pierce with decorated cocktail toothpicks for serving. Serves a small gathering.

Keys Cup
~ Florida Keys ~

3 cups assorted melon balls   4 cups orange and grapefruit sections   3 cups avocado balls
whipped cream   seedless grapes

Gently toss all ingredients into a large bowl. Portion into festive dessert cups and top with whipped cream. Accent with grapes. Serves 16-20.

Nassau Hot Crab Appetizers
~ Bahamas ~

1 (6.5) ounce can crab meat, drained   1 tablespoon milk   1 teaspoon hot sauce
2 tablespoons onion, minced   1 teaspoon horseradish   dash paprika
1 tablespoon Worcestershire sauce   dash salt   dash freshly ground pepper
1 (8) ounce package cream cheese, softened

Heat oven to 350°F. In a large mixing bowl, combine together all ingredients except paprika. Place in baking dish and accent with paprika. Bake in oven 20-30 minutes. Serve immediately with crackers. Serves 4.

Oyster Cocktail
~ Puerto Rico ~

24 oysters, removed from shell   1 tablespoon fresh lime juice   1 cup tomato ketchup
1 teaspoon fresh coriander, crushed   dash salt   dash freshly ground pepper
¼ cup water   ¼ teaspoon hot pepper, crushed

Mix all of the ingredients together except oysters. Let stand for 1 hour. Divide oysters between two glasses. Fill with the sauce and serve. Serves 2.

Pan de Ajo
~ Puerto Rico ~

1 French baguette or Italian loaf
dash olive oil

2 garlic cloves, crushed
2 tablespoons butter

dash dried oregano
dash freshly ground pepper

Prepare a 350°F oven and cut bread lengthwise. Sprinkle each cut side with a layer of garlic. Brush with olive oil and dot with butter. Sprinkle with oregano and pepper. Wrap in foil and bake for 15 minutes. Remove foil and cut into 2 inch slices. Serve hot.

Phlourie
~ Guyana ~

2 cups split pea flour or besan
½ teaspoon turmeric
2 cloves garlic, minced
2 cups vegetable oil for deep frying
1 green onion (only green part) chopped fine

1 cup self rising flour
½ teaspoon cumin
½ small onion, minced
¼ teaspoon hot pepper, seeded, minced

¼ teaspoon baking powder
1 teaspoon salt
⅔ cup water

Sift both flours and baking powder into a mixing bowl. Stir in remaining dry ingredients. Add enough water to form a very thick batter. Mix in onions, garlic, green onion and hot pepper. Heat oil in a deep saucepan until about 375°F. Drop mixture in by tablespoons and fry until all sides are golden brown. Drain on paper towels and serve warm. Makes 36.

Souskai d' Avocats
~ Martinique ~

2 just ripened avocados
1 seeded and chopped hot chile pepper

1 garlic clove, minced

dash salt
2 juiced limes

Trim avocados and cut flesh into small cubes. Grind the salt and garlic into a paste. Add the chile and continue grinding. Finally, stir in lime juice. Marinate avocado bits for 1 hour. Serve with decorative toothpicks.

St. John's Coconut Mussels
~ U.S. Virgin Islands ~

1 tablespoon olive oil
4 ounces creamed coconut
1 teaspoon sugar
1 teaspoon fresh thyme

2 shallots, minced
½ cup dry white wine
dash salt
2 pounds mussels, cleaned well

1 garlic clove, crushed
⅓ cup of heavy cream
dash freshly ground pepper
thyme sprigs, to garnish

Scrub down the mussels and pull off the "beards". Discard broken ones, or those that pop open easily with a sharp tap. Sauté garlic and shallots in oil for 5 minutes in a large saucepan. Slowly portion in creamed coconut and follow with cream, sugar, wine, thyme and seasoning. Boil and reduce to a simmer for 5 minutes. Place mussels into skillet and cook for 5 minutes in sauce until they open. Garnish with thyme sprigs. Serves 4.

Stamp and Go (Fish Fritters)
~ Jamaica ~

8 ounces salt cod, soaked overnight | 1 cup flour (self rising) | 1 egg, beaten
¾ cup milk | 1 tablespoon butter, melted | 1 tablespoon vegetable oil
1 hot pepper, seeded and minced | 1 onion, minced | vegetable oil, for frying
lemon wedges, to garnish

Sift together flour and salt. Blend egg, milk, and melted butter. Add into flour and stir until smooth. Set aside. Rinse salt cod well and drain. Place into a saucepan with enough cold water to cover fish. Bring to a boil. Then simmer, covered, for 20 minutes or until fish is tender. Drain off water and allow to cool. Clean off any excess and bones. Flake fish. Sauté onion in oil until soft. Add the fish, onion and pepper into the batter. Heat ½ inch of oil in a frying pan. Using a teaspoon portion, drop batter into frying pan, cooking only a few at a time, until golden and crispy on both sides. Drain. Accompany with lemon wedges. Serves 6.

Stuffed Breadfruit
~ Jamaica ~

2 cups assorted, chopped vegetables or 3 cups washed spinach | 1 whole breadfruit
½ cup blended tomato or prepared tomato sauce | dash salt
dash freshly ground pepper

Prepare a 350°F oven. Core and remove stem from a washed breadfruit. Blend together tomato and vegetable mixture with seasoning to taste. Stuff the breadfruit. Place in a pan with 1 inch of water. Put in oven and bake until tender, about 1 hour. Remove when done and cool. Peel and cut into wedges with vegetable portions intact. Serves 4.

Stuffed Crab Backs
~ Dominica ~

4 small, dressed crabs (12 ounces each) | | 1 tablespoon fresh lime juice
1½ cups fresh white bread crumbs | ¼ cup butter | 3 tablespoons dark rum
1 onion, minced | 2 garlic cloves, crushed | dash salt
dash ground pepper | 1 hot pepper, seeded and minced | ¼ teaspoon nutmeg, grated
2 tablespoons fresh chives, chopped | 2 tablespoons fresh parsley, chopped | 2 sprigs thyme, chopped fine
lemon wedges, to garnish

Bring a large pot of water to a boil. Drop crabs in and boil for 10 minutes. Remove when cooked and drain. Take out meat and save the cleaned crab backs. Sauté onion in medium frying pan with half the butter. In a bowl, mix together crabmeat, 1 cup of breadcrumbs, water, crabmeat, chives, garlic, lime juice, pepper, thyme, parsley, rum, nutmeg, salt and pepper. Preheat oven to 350°F. Stuff crab backs with crab mixture and sprinkle each with left over breadcrumbs. Dot butter on top and bake about 20 minutes or until golden brown. Serves 4.

Tannia Fritters
~ St. Nevis ~

4-6 tannias
1 tablespoon butter
½ cup vegetable oil

2 cups salted water
1 garlic clove, pressed

2 eggs
dash salt

Peel tannias and boil in salted water until soft. Drain water. Add butter, salt, garlic and eggs. Mash into a thick consistency. Heat vegetable oil in a deep pan. When hot, spoon in tannia batter and fry until golden brown. Serves 4.

Titiri Ackra
~ Dominica ~

2 pounds titiri, washed and drained
1½ ounces garlic, chopped

1½ cups flour
2 teaspoons salt

3 hot red peppers

In a bowl, place all ingredients and mix thoroughly. Heat oil for deep-frying in a large pan until extremely hot. Spoon small amount of mixture into the oil. Fry until browned and drain on paper towels. Serve with pepper sauce. Makes 12.

Tostones
~ Cuba ~

3 green plantains, peeled and sliced diagonally into 1 inch pieces
2 cups vegetable oil, for deep frying

2 cups water
2 teaspoons salt

In a bowl, mix water and salt. Put plantain slices into the salted water and allow to stand for 10 minutes. In a deep frying pan, heat oil to about 360°F. Drain plantains and fry until tender (not crisp), about 8 minutes. Remove from pan with a slotted utensil and place pieces on layered paper towel, and press to flatten (try using a bottle filled with liquid). Return slices to oil and fry again, this time until golden brown and crisp, approximately 5-6 minutes. Drain again on paper towels and serve hot. Serves 4.

Virgin Lobster Stew
~ Virgin Islands ~

2 lobster tails, 1 pound each, sliced
1 small can peeled tomatoes
1 onion, chopped
1 tablespoon olive oil
dash freshly ground pepper

½ pound butternut squash, boiled, and sliced
6 small potatoes, peeled, boiled and sliced
¼ pound carrots, peeled, boiled, and sliced
1 green pepper, seeded and chopped   dash salt
½ can green peas, drained   1 cup white wine

In a deep pot, warm olive oil over medium heat. Put green pepper and onion in pot and sauté for few seconds. Add lobster slices and sauté for 5 minutes. Add salt, pepper and tomatoes. Sauté mixture for 2 minutes. Add in the rest of the ingredients. Simmer 3 minutes making sure lobster meat is cooked. Serve hot. Serves 2.

Soups

Bayan Banana Peanut Soup
~ Barbados ~

2 cups chicken stock
1-2 tablespoons hot pepper sauce

½ cup crunchy peanut butter
½ cup shredded coconut, toasted

3 mashed bananas

Heat chicken broth over moderate heat and stir in peanut butter until smooth. Add bananas and season with hot sauce as desired. Garnish with toasted coconut.

Breadfruit Soup
~ Trinidad ~

8 ounces of either: salted beef, salted pig tail, corned beef, chopped ham or smoked ham hock
1 yellow breadfruit, cored, peeled and sliced
1 sprig thyme
1 hot pepper, whole
chopped parsley for garnish

2 green onions, chopped
6 cups water

4 cups coconut milk
1 medium onion, chopped
dash salt

Boil meat in water for approximately 1 hour or until tender. Drain and reserve the stock. Cut meat into small bite-size pieces and set aside. In a large saucepan, add reserved stock and breadfruit. Boil for about 15-20 minutes or until tender. In a food processor or blender, purée breadfruit with ⅓ cup of the stock. Return to pan adding coconut milk, onions, hot pepper, thyme and salt to taste. Simmer on low for 15 minutes. Remove hot pepper and thyme before serving. Serve piping hot with a garnish of fresh parsley. Serves 4-6.

Callaloo Soup
~ Dominica ~

4 ounces salt pork
4 ounces crabmeat
1 stalk celery with leaves chopped
dash salt
½ cup coconut milk
4 cups water
8 ounces callaloo leaves, cleaned, stemmed and chopped (can substitute with spinach or bok choy)

6 okras, washed
3 sprigs fresh parsley, chopped
2 whole cloves
dash ground black pepper
2 whole scallions, chopped

1 ounce dried shrimp
½ teaspoon dried thyme
1 small onion, chopped
1 garlic clove, minced
1 green onion, chopped

In heavy saucepan, cover salt meat with 3 cups of water. Bring to a boil and continue to boil for 1 hour or until meat is almost tender. Soak shrimp in 1 cup of water. Drain and add to saucepan with meat. Add remaining ingredients and simmer for about 45 minutes. Remove meat when tender and chop into small pieces. Return to mixture and add coconut milk, crabmeat, pepper and salt. Simmer for 5 minutes to combine flavors. Purée mixture in a blender or food processor until smooth. Return to saucepan and reheat. Serves 4.

Coconut-Shrimp Soup
~ St. Vincent ~

½ pound shrimp, peeled
½ teaspoon roasted coriander seeds
1½ piece fresh ginger, shredded
sprig basil, finely chopped

1 cup coconut milk
1 cup chicken stock
1 sprig lemon grass

3 garlic cloves
½ lime, zest
¼ hot pepper, seeded

Bring all the ingredients to a boil except for shrimp and basil. Simmer for 15 minutes. Add shrimp and cook for 3 minutes. Garnish with fresh basil. Serves 2.

Cool Breeze Gazpacho
~ Puerto Rico ~

1 green bell pepper, chopped
½ teaspoon of salt
¾ cup chicken broth
2 tablespoons vinegar, red wine variety

5 tomatoes, halved, seeded and chopped
3 cucumbers, peeled, seeded and diced
¼ teaspoon cayenne

1 chopped onion
1 crushed garlic clove
3 tablespoons olive oil

Blend together all ingredients in a food processor or similar, while reserving the olive oil to the side. Whisk the olive oil into the puréed vegetable blend in a large bowl. Cover with plastic wrap and chill for 2 hours. Makes 6 portions.

Creamed Garbanzo Bean Soup
~ Curaçao ~

8 ounces chickpeas, soaked overnight and drained
2 garlic cloves, crushed
½ teaspoon cumin

1 onion, finely chopped
dash salt

5 cups water
½ teaspoon white pepper
¾ cup evaporated milk

Place chickpeas and water in large saucepan. Cook peas for about 40 minutes or just until tender. Add remaining ingredients except evaporated milk. Cook an additional 40 minutes until chickpeas are soft, not mushy. Add evaporated milk and simmer on low for 6 minutes. Remove soup and purée in blender. Return to pan and stir for 3-4 minutes over low heat. Serve hot. Serves 4.

Duval Street Chilled Avocado Soup
~ Key West, Florida ~

2 avocados, ripe, peeled and seeded
1 tablespoon lime juice
dash salt

1 garlic clove, crushed
1 tablespoon sour cream
dash freshly ground pepper

3 cups chicken stock
3 chives, chopped finely
dash hot pepper sauce

In a blender, purée half of the chicken stock, avocado, lime juice, garlic, sour cream, salt and pepper. Mix in remaining stock until smooth. Stir in hot pepper sauce. Chill for minimum of 1 hour. Before serving, garnish with chives. Serves 4.

Eddo Soup
~ Barbuda ~

2 pounds eddo (tarro root)
4 ounces celery, chopped
4 ounces onions, chopped
dash salt
4 ounces leeks, chopped

2 sprigs thyme
2 cloves
1 garlic clove, chopped
dash freshly ground pepper

4 ounces leeks, chopped
4 cups chicken stock
½ hot red pepper, chopped
2 bay leaves

Peel and slice eddoes. Add all ingredients in a large pot of water and bring to a boil. Season with salt and pepper. Skim foam off the top. Simmer on low heat for 40 minutes. Remove from heat. Pour in a blender and blend on high until smooth. Pour through a strainer. Pour into soup bowls. Sprinkle with paprika as a garnish. Serves 4.

Fish Chowder
~ Key Largo ~

2 pounds nonoily fish heads
dash salt
6 cups water
1 celery stalk, sliced
⅛ teaspoon ground nutmeg
1 tomato, peeled and chopped
1 small hot red pepper, seeded and minced

1 pound red snapper fillets
½ teaspoon white pepper
1 carrot, diced
2 sprigs thyme
1 tablespoon tomato purée
1-2 tablespoons of sherry

1 tablespoon Key lime juice
½ teaspoon paprika
1 onion, diced
2 bay leaves
chopped fresh parsley

Sprinkle cleaned fish heads with Key lime juice. Cut fish fillets into 2 inch pieces and season with paprika, salt and white pepper. Place fish heads into boiling water in a large pan and simmer for 30 minutes. Strain broth and discard fish heads. Add carrot, onion, celery, tomato paste, herbs and spices to broth and simmer for 20 minutes. Add in prepared fish pieces and cook an additional 10 minutes. Flavor with sherry and garnish with parsley. Serves 4-6.

Freeport Land Crab Soup
~ Bahamas ~

6 large white land crabs, washed
3 tablespoons tomato purée
¼ cup rice
8 cups boiling water

2 tablespoons olive oil
1 tablespoon all-purpose flour
2 potatoes, quartered

1 large onion, chopped
1 teaspoon thyme
2 large carrots, cut in chunks

For 20 minutes cook uncracked crabs in 2 tablespoons of water over a low heat until water is evaporated and shells are red. Turn crabs over, so as no to burn. When cooked, remove and crack shells, separating out the meat and discarding the shells. Sauté onion, tomato purée, flour and thyme in oil in a large pot. Stir until onions are glazed. Add in meat and claws and continue stirring for one more minute. Add chopped vegetables and rice along with boiling water. On low heat, simmer for 2 hours. Serves 6.

Gazpacho
~ Cuba ~

3 medium cucumbers, peeled, seeded and diced
3 large tomatoes, split in half, seeds squeezed out, and chopped
1 large green bell pepper, seeded and chopped
1 garlic clove, peeled and crushed   2 tablespoons red wine vinegar

1 large onion, chopped
dash salt
3 tablespoons olive oil
¾ cup chicken broth

Purée all ingredients except olive oil in a food processor or blender. Pour into a bowl and stir in the olive oil. Refrigerate for at least 3 hours before serving. Serves 6.

Giraumon Soup
~ Haiti ~

1 pound salted beef
2 green onions, finely chopped
2 garlic cloves, crushed
1 tablespoon butter
dash freshly ground pepper

1½ pound pumpkin, peeled and diced
1 sprig fresh thyme
1 cup milk
¾ cup rice, washed

1 small onion, finely chopped
1 sprig fresh parsley
⅛ teaspoon ground nutmeg
dash salt

In a saucepan, place salted beef with water to cover generously. Bring to a boil and continue to cook partially covered on medium-low heat for 1 hour. Drain liquid and chop meat into small pieces. In a medium saucepan, boil 4 cups of water. Add beef pieces, pumpkin, parsley onions, thyme and 1 garlic clove. Simmer for about 15 minutes or until pumpkin is tender. Remove parsley and thyme. Place pumpkin into a food processor or blender with ¼ cup of the stock. Purée and then return to the saucepan. Heat thoroughly. Add butter, milk, rice and nutmeg. Cook for about 15-20 minutes or until rice is tender. Add salt and pepper to taste. Stir in remaining garlic. Serve piping hot with a small pat of butter. Serves 4.

Island-Style Avocado Soup
~ Key West ~

2 ripe avocados, peeled and cubed
1 tablespoon Key lime juice
1 tablespoon sour cream

1 garlic clove, crushed
dash salt
½ teaspoon hot pepper sauce

3 cups chicken broth
dash freshly ground pepper
3 chives, minced

In a food processor or blender, combine avocado, garlic, Key lime juice, sour cream, half of chicken broth, salt and pepper to a puréed consistency. Add in remaining chicken stock and blend until smooth. Stir in hot pepper sauce to accent flavor. Chill for one hour and garnish soup with chives before presentation. Serves 4.

Orange Consommé
~ Grenada ~

2 envelopes gelatin, unflavored
1 orange, unpeeled, cut crosswise into thin slices
1 quart cold chicken stock, fresh or canned

2 egg whites, beaten to a froth

dash salt
3 cups orange juice, strained

First, skim the surface of the chicken stock removing all fat. Then, pour into a bowl and add gelatin on top. Let soften for 5 minutes. Pour stock in a large saucepan and add eggs. Bring to a boil on high heat stirring with a whisk constantly. When stock begins to rise, remove from heat and allow to cool down. Pour through double-thick cheesecloth or a dampened kitchen towel. Allow the liquid to drain through into a bowl without disturbing at any point. Add in salt and strained orange juice and stir. Refrigerate for 6 hours until thoroughly chilled and firm. Serve and garnish with slices of orange. Serves 6.

Papaya Soup
~ Jamaica ~

1 fully ripe medium papaya

1 tablespoon sugar

1 lime, juiced

Peel and cut up papaya. Save seeds in container and refrigerate. In a blender, mix to a fine liquid the papaya, lime juice and sugar. Mix in a little water if soup is too thick. Serve chilled. Garnish with a cluster of seeds.

Pepperpot
~ Guyana ~

4 cups water
8 ounces oxtail or choice, as desired
½ teaspoon ginger, grated
sprigs thyme, chopped
dash freshly ground pepper

2½ pounds lean meat (chicken, pork, beef, or duck), chopped
2 teaspoons raw sugar
4 garlic cloves
2 whole red hot peppers
½ cup cassareep (see page: 18)

1 stick cinnamon
2 whole cloves
dash salt

Boil water in a medium saucepan. Toss in all ingredients and add enough water to cover meat. Bring to a simmer and cook until meat is soft, around 2 hours. Remove hot pepper before serving. Serves 6.

Sopa de Gandules
~ Puerto Rico ~

1 cup onions, chopped
4 ounces lean salt pork, diced
1 teaspoon garlic, chopped
1 pound West Indian Pumpkin, peeled, seeded and diced (can substitute with winter squash or Hubbard)
1 large ripe tomato, peeled, seeded and chopped or ½ cup chopped drained canned tomato
4 ounces lean boneless cooked ham, diced

1 can green pigeon peas, with liquid
1 green bell pepper, seeded and chopped
dash freshly ground pepper

1 quart chicken stock

dash salt

In a heavy saucepan, fry the salt pork until crispy and brown and have rendered all their fat. Remove pork and dice. Place back into saucepan. Add in garlic and onions to the fat and stir. Cook for 5 minutes until they are soft and transparent. Add ham, green pepper and tomato cover and simmer 5 more minutes. Pour in stock, add pumpkin and green pigeon peas into saucepan. Bring to a boil and reduce heat, cover and simmer for 20 minutes until soup thickens and pumpkin is soft. Add salt and pepper. Soup should be lumpy. Serves 6.

Sopa de Pollo
~ Cuba ~

2 pounds chicken parts
2 onions, sliced
2 ripe tomatoes, chopped finely
¼ teaspoon dried oregano or 2 teaspoons fresh, chopped finely
2 green plantains peeled, sliced 1¼ inch thick
8 ounces sweet potato, peeled and cubed
8 ounces pumpkin, cleaned, peeled and cubed

10 cups water
2 tablespoons tomato paste
1 stalk celery, chopped

2 garlic cloves, crushed
4 ounces carrots, diced
dash salt
1 chicken bullion cube
1 tablespoon butter
½ teaspoon cumin
8 ounces yuca peeled, cubed

In a large saucepan, bring the water to a boil. Add chicken and salt. Cook on medium heat about 20 minutes, or until chicken is tender. Add garlic, onions, oregano, tomatoes, tomato paste and celery. Simmer for 10 minutes. Add remaining ingredients except noodles, butter and cumin. Cook over low heat about 40-45 minutes, or until vegetables are tender. Add noodles, butter and cumin. Cover and cook about 4-6 minutes, or until noodles are tender. Serve hot. Serves 4.

Southernmost Point Conch Chowder
~ Key West, Florida ~

¼ cup bacon or salt pork, diced finely
2 finely chopped onions
2 medium green peppers, diced
5 ripe but firm tomatoes (can substitute with 1 can of peeled tomatoes)
6 conches, pounded well and diced

1 garlic clove
1 teaspoon paprika
2 celery stalks, sliced finely

dash freshly ground pepper

½ thyme sprig
3 potatoes, diced
¼ cup tomato paste
dash Sherry
dash salt

In a Dutch oven, fry bacon or salt pork until golden brown. Add peppers, celery, onions, thyme and garlic. Cook until soft. Add tomatoes, tomato paste, conch, 2 cups of water and potatoes. Bring to a boil. Add enough water to cover mixture. Simmer for 25 minutes. Make sure there is always sufficient water in pot. Add dash of sherry for zest at the end of cooking. Serves 4-6.

Sunny Pumpkin Soup
~ Jamaica ~

2 pounds pumpkin, peeled, seeded and cubed
1 tablespoon lime juice   1 large onion, chopped
14 ounce can coconut milk   1 celery stick, finely chopped
¼ teaspoon grated nutmeg   1 small red chili, seeded and chopped
toasted coconut flakes and lime rind, to garnish

2 tablespoons butter
3¾ cups chicken stock
dash salt
dash ground pepper

Heat butter in a large saucepan. Add onion and celery, cooking for 10 minutes until soft. Add pumpkin, chili, stock, coconut milk, lime juice and seasoning. Bring to a boil. Cover and simmer on medium heat for 20-30 minutes until pumpkin is soft. Purée soup and return to saucepan. Reheat soup and stir in nutmeg. Serve in soup bowls and garnish with coconut flakes and lime rind. Serves 6.

Sweet Potato and Tomato Soup
~ Barbados ~

1 tablespoon olive oil   1 tablespoon butter   2 onions, minced
2 celery stalks, sliced thin   1 cup sweet potatoes, diced   1 orange, juiced
14 ounce can chopped tomatoes   1 orange rind grated
3¾ cups vegetable or chicken broth   1 teaspoon fresh oregano, chopped
½ teaspoon fresh thyme, chopped   dash freshly ground pepper   dash salt

Garnish: sour cream   orange rind   cayenne red pepper
2 teaspoons salt

In a pan, cook celery and onions in oil and butter for 10 minutes. Add in stock or broth, sweet potatoes, tomatoes, orange juice and rind, herbs and spices. Bring to a boil. Reduce heat and then simmer covered for 20 minutes until sweet potatoes are tender. Purée soup in a blender in portions. Heat up again and serve. Garnish with a circular form of sour cream topped with a shower of orange rind, salt and a dust of cayenne. Serves 6.

Taino Seafood Stew
~ Haiti ~

¼ pound crabmeat   ½ pound whelks   ½ pound lobster, in the shell
½ pound shrimp, in the shell   ½ pound oysters   ½ pound clams, in the shell
¼ pound river crawfish, in the shell   2 ears sweet corn, cut into pieces   1 teaspoon ground annatto
2 tomatoes, chopped   1 tablespoon vegetable oil   ½ cup coconut milk
1 hot pepper   2 limes, juiced

In a large earthenware pot, heat oil. Add the annatto, then add all ingredients and stir. Cover with ½ cup water and coconut milk. Place red pepper in a small gauze bag and then immerse in stew along with lime juice. Cook 25-35 minutes. Serves 4.

Salads

Banana-Strawberry Salad
~ Grenada ~

3 sliced bananas, ½ inch thick
1 cup quartered strawberries

1 cantaloupe, cut with melon baller
½ cup fresh orange juice

1 cup sour cream
½ cup grenadine syrup

Mix together fruit and orange juice in a bowl. Portion into serving bowls. Blend together sour cream and grenadine into a small bowl. Ladle over fruit cups and garnish with mint leaves.

Black Bean Salad
~ Dominican Republic ~

1 tablespoon chopped almonds
½ cup mango, peeled and diced
1 tablespoon almonds, chopped
2 tablespoons each of red, yellow, and green bell pepper, chopped
dash freshly ground pepper

1 cup canned black beans
½ cup papaya, peeled, seeded and diced
2 tablespoons fresh parsley

¼ teaspoon hot pepper, seeded and chopped

1 tablespoon raisins
2 tablespoons lime juice
2 tablespoons olive oil
dash salt

Mix fruits, peppers and beans in a large bowl. In a small bowl, mix lime juice and vegetable oil. Pour over salad. Sprinkle with almonds, raisins and parsley. Serves 4.

Cayo Hueso Key Lime Salad
~ Key West, Florida Keys ~

½ cup fresh orange juice
2 tablespoons orange peel, grated
2 grapefruits, peeled, sectioned

2 tablespoons lime juice
2 tangerines, peeled, seeded, sectioned
4 oranges, peeled, seedless, sectioned

1 cup sugar
2 teaspoons lime peel, grated
3 Key limes, peeled, sectioned

Dissolve sugar into orange and lime juice in a small saucepan over a moderate heat. Turn off heat and cool with grated orange and lime peels. In a separate bowl, lightly toss together fruit. Stir in prepared syrup. Chill for 1 hour. Serves 8.

Conch Salad
~ Key West, Florida Keys ~

1 pound conch meat, pounded and minced
½ onion, finely sliced
2 peeled tomatoes, peeled and diced
1 tablespoon fresh parsley, chopped

¼ cucumber, diced
½ hot red pepper, seeded and diced

4 Key limes, juiced
½ celery stalk, diced
½ romaine lettuce bunch

Rinse conch meat with limewater and pound with a mallet to double its size. Place in bowl with Key lime juice and add all ingredients except lettuce and parsley. Mix well. Marinate for 1 hour in the refrigerator. Serve on lettuce leaves in an attractive salad bowl and top with parsley. Serves 6.

Curried-Coconut Lobster Salad
~ St. Vincent ~

1 pound cooked lobster tail meat   1 head bib lettuce, washed and leaves separated
dash red pepper sauce   6 tablespoons mayonnaise   1 teaspoon coconut cream
1 tomato, sliced   1 teaspoon lime juice   ½ overripe avocado, peeled

On 4 plates arrange lettuce and tomato slices. Place lobster on the dishes. In a blender, add coconut cream, hot sauce, lime juice, mayonnaise and avocado and liquefy. Pour dressing over salad.

Ensalada de Chayote
~ Puerto Rico ~

2 cups cherry tomatoes, sliced   3 chayotes, peeled and cut lengthwise   1 cluster watercress
¼ cup pitted olives, sliced in half

Dressing: 6 tablespoons olive oil   2 tablespoons red wine vinegar   2 garlic cloves, crushed
¼ teaspoon fresh oregano   dash freshly ground pepper   dash salt

Put chayotes in a pan covered by 1 inch of water. Cook until tender. Drain and remove seeds. Chop into chunks. Rinse and trim watercress. Pat dry and place in a serving bowl along with chayotes, tomatoes and olives. Mix together all ingredients for dressing and shake well in a sealed container. Pour over salad, toss lightly and serve. Serves 6.

Ensalada de Aguacate y Jueyes
~ Puerto Rico ~

1 pound fresh lump crabmeat   1 cup mayonnaise   1 lemon, halved
2 tablespoons onion, minced   1 garlic clove, crushed   ¼ cup parsley, diced
¼ teaspoon dried oregano   dash freshly ground pepper   dash salt
2 avocados   2 trimmed tomatoes, cut in wedges

Garnish: parsley sprigs

Remove any shell from crabmeat. In a large bowl, add crab, mayonnaise, juice of half a lemon, seasoning, onion, garlic and parsley. Cut avocado in half, remove pit and peel. Cut into 6-8 wedges and sprinkle with juice from the remaining lemon half. Place crabmeat salad in the center of a serving platter. Decorate with alternate wedges of tomato and avocado. Lightly sprinkle with salt and accent with clusters of parsley. Serves 4.

Ensalada de Pulpo
~ Dominican Republic ~

3 young octopuses, 2 pounds each
3 garlic cloves, peeled
¾ cup olive oil
½ teaspoon dried sage
6 pimiento stuffed Spanish olives

1 teaspoon salt
½ teaspoon dried oregano
2 teaspoons vinegar
1 onion, sliced into thin rings
1 tomato, cut into thin wedges

½ lemon, juiced
½ teaspoon salt
dash freshly ground pepper

Rinse and drain octopus in cold water. Trim off the mouth and pouch underneath the body and discard. Place in large pot, covered with salted water. Bring to a boil. Then simmer covered for 25-30 minutes. The meat is pink and tender when cooked. Remove from heat and allow 10 minutes for cooling. Drain off water. Trim off top of heads. Flush head cavity. Trim off tentacles and scrape skin. Cut octopus meat into bite-sized pieces. Put in a bowl with juice from the lemon half. Crush garlic in with salt and oregano. Add in vinegar and rub mixture onto chunks of meat. Pour olive oil blended with sage and pepper over the top of the octopus pieces. Include olives and onions and toss. Cover and refrigerate for at least 1 hour before serving. Garnish with tomatoes. Serves 4-6.

Festival Rice Salad
~ Jamaica ~

1⅓ cups long grain rice
1 red bell pepper, halved
1 hot pepper, seeded and minced
¾ cup cashews, roasted and salted
½ orange, juiced and rind grated

dash freshly ground pepper
1 yellow bell pepper, halved
flesh of ½ coconut, coarsely grated
fresh chives, chopped, to garnish

dash salt
⅓ cup raisins
⅔ cup mayonnaise
1 banana, sliced

Cook rice in salted boiling water for 10-15 minutes until just soft. Rinse and drain in cool water. On a preheated grill, broil pepper halves, with the skin side up, until blackened. Set aside in a plastic bag to cool. Peel off skins and cut into strips. In a mixing bowl, combine raisins, cashews, coconut, hot pepper, broiled peppers and cooked rice. In a side bowl, stir together mayonnaise with orange juice and rind. Fold orange mayonnaise into rice blend. Gently toss in sliced banana. Spoon into a decorative bowl and accent with chives. Serves 6.

Flying Fish Salad
~ Barbados ~

5 flying fish, cleaned
2½ ounces cream cheese
1 tablespoon mayonnaise

½ onion, chopped
½ Scotch Bonnet hot red pepper, seeded and chopped
½ lime juice

dash salt

2 teaspoons pepper sauce

Poach fish for 5 minutes then mash with fingers into a bowl. Set aside ¼ red hot pepper and onion for garnishing. Add remaining ingredients in bowl with fish and mix well. Place in the refrigerator to chill. Serve with toasted bread or on a bed of greens. Garnish on one side with red hot pepper and onion. Serves 4.

Haitian Bananes Jaunes au Gratin des Deux Fromages
~ Haiti ~

6 very ripe bananas
¼ cup grated gruyere cheese
dash freshly ground pepper

¼ cup butter
2 cups milk
dash salt

¼ cup flour
dash nutmeg, freshly grated

Preheat oven to 400°F. Place bananas in a pot and add water, covering bananas. Cook on medium heat for 15 minutes or until tender. Remove bananas, peel them and cut bananas into pieces. Place in a casserole dish. To make béchamel sauce, heat butter and flour in a saucepan on low heat. Gently pour in milk and seasonings. Stir constantly until a thick sauce forms. Add half of the cheese to sauce. Pour the béchamel over bananas. Sprinkle the rest of the cheese on top of the dish and bake for 20 minutes. Serves 4.

Hearts of Palm Salad
~ Dominican Republic ~

½ pound hearts of palm
1 yellow bell pepper, chopped
4 tablespoons tarragon vinegar
dash freshly ground black pepper

4 tablespoons olive oil
1 green bell pepper, chopped
1 small head of lettuce (torn into pieces)

½ garlic clove
1 red sweet pepper, chopped

Cut the hearts of palm into ½ inch pieces. Marinate with vinegar. Refrigerate over night. Drain and set the vinegar aside. Rub garlic around the inside of a wooden salad bowl. Add the lettuce, hearts of the palm and peppers. Toss the salad. In a small bowl, mix olive oil, black pepper, vinegar and a dash of salt. Pour over salad. Garnish with parsley. Serves 2.

Mama's Best Blue Marlin Salad
~ St. Vincent ~

1 pound blue marlin or tuna steaks
1 cup minced celery

2 cups peeled, diced pumpkin
1 lemon, quartered

8 broccoli florets, blanched
1 bunch lettuce

Curry Mayonnaise: 1 teaspoon Dijon-style mustard
2 tablespoons lemon juice
2 garlic cloves, minced
¼ teaspoon turmeric

1 tablespoon minced fresh ginger
1 tablespoon curry powder
¼ teaspoon cayenne pepper

1 egg yolk
¾ cup olive oil
¼ teaspoon ground cloves
¼ teaspoon salt

Cook fish steaks in boiling water for 10 minutes. Drain, shred and refrigerate for 1 hour. Boil pumpkin in water for 10 minutes. Drain and refrigerate for 1 hour. For mayonnaise, blend egg yolk for 15 seconds in a food processor or blender. Add mustard and lemon juice. Process for an additional 10 seconds. While motor is on, slowly drizzle in olive oil. Stop and scrape the sides when half of the oil remains. Add remaining ingredients making sure to incorporate well. For salad assembly: combine in a large bowl, curry mayonnaise, fish, broccoli, celery and pumpkin. Toss and serve on a bed of lettuce or use as a sandwich filling. Squeeze lemon over the salad before serving. Makes 4 servings.

Mango Cucumber Salad
~ Key West, Florida Keys ~

1 small ripe mango, peeled, cut from the pit and sliced
1 large cucumber, peeled, seeded and cut into ¼ inch slices
1 avocado, peeled, pitted and sliced
2 tablespoons freshly squeezed Key lime juice
¼ cup fresh mint, cut into julienne pieces

1 cup cherry tomatoes
½ cup bean sprouts
¼ cup rice vinegar
2 teaspoons sugar

In a bowl, toss the cucumber, tomatoes, green beans and bean sprouts together. Cover and place in the refrigerator for 1-4 hours. In another bowl, mix the vinegar, Key lime juice and sugar. Stir until the sugar dissolves. Arrange the salad mixture, avocado and mango slices on salad plates. Sprinkle with the dressing and garnish with the mint. Serves 4.

Marathon Shrimp Grapefruit Salad
~ Florida Keys ~

1 cup grapefruit sections, chopped
1 cup shrimp, boiled and chopped
1 red bell pepper, seeded and diced

1 cup cucumbers, diced
¾ cup celery, diced

1 cup mayonnaise
romaine lettuce

Blend together shrimp with grapefruit, cucumber, celery and mayonnaise. Allow to chill before serving. Arrange crisp lettuce on to salad plates. Scoop shrimp mix onto lettuce. Garnish with pimiento.

Papaya and Avocado Salad
~ Cayman Islands ~

1 large papaya

2 avocados, peeled and sliced lengthwise

Dressing: 2 tablespoons lime juice
1 fresh red chili, seeded and finely chopped
dash freshly ground pepper

1 teaspoon sugar

dash salt

¼ cup virgin olive oil
1 teaspoon Dijon mustard

Peel papaya and avocados and cut lengthwise. Remove papaya seeds and reserve. Thinly slice papaya and avocados.

Dressing: Whisk in a bowl, lime juice, sugar, olive oil, chili, mustard and seasoning. Pour over salad. Garnish with papaya seeds if desired. Serves 4.

Papaya Tropicale
~ Key Largo, Florida Keys ~

4 cups ripe papaya cut in cubes
¾ cup mayonnaise

6 teaspoons finely chopped onion
1 cup finely chopped celery

1 teaspoon salt

Cut papaya into cubes, add chopped onion and celery. Chill. Serve on lettuce leaves and garnish with mayonnaise.

Pineapple Shrimp Cool-Me-Down Salad
~ Key West, Florida Keys ~

¾ pound peeled and deveined cooked shrimp
2 oranges

1 avocado

1 pineapple
1 tablespoon orange juice

Chill shrimp. Cut pineapple lengthwise. Remove core and meat. Reserve shell for serving. Dice pineapple. Peel and section oranges, reserve juice. Cut avocado in half lengthwise and remove seed. Peel and slice avocado. Sprinkle with orange juice to prevent discoloration. Combine pineapple, oranges and avocado. Fill pineapple shells with fruit mixture. Arrange shrimp on top. Serves 2.

Rasta Salad
~ Jamaica ~

½ cup red kidney beans, cooked
½ cup black-eyed beans, cooked
1 yellow bell pepper, cut in slices
4 tablespoons sesame or peanut oil
dash freshly ground pepper

1 garlic clove
1 green bell pepper, cut in slices
¼ cup coconut, fresh grated
1 lime, freshly squeezed
1 teaspoon malt vinegar

1 red bell pepper, cut in slices
1 tablespoon raisins
1 tablespoon chopped nuts
1 teaspoon brown cane sugar

Cut garlic in half and rub into wooden salad bowl making sure the strong garlic smell emanates from the bowl. Then, add black-eyed beans, kidney beans, coconut, chopped nuts, bell peppers and raisins. Pour the sesame or peanut oil in another bowl. Add lime juice, sugar, black pepper and malt vinegar. Pour over salad and toss. Serves 4.

Saint Lucian Grapefruit-Avocado Salad
~ Saint Lucia ~

2 pink grapefruits
1 tablespoon fresh grapefruit juice
¼ teaspoon freshly ground allspice

2 ripe avocados
¼ cup light olive oil
candied grapefruit

1 tablespoon cane vinegar
parsley sprigs

Slice avocado lengthwise, remove pits and peel them. Segment grapefruit removing all of the membrane. Reserve 1 tablespoon of juice. From remaining ingredients, prepare vinaigrette including grapefruit juice. On a salad plate, arrange grapefruit and avocado in alternating bands. Pour vinaigrette over. Garnish with pieces of candied grapefruit rind and sprig of parsley. Serves 4.

Stone Crab Salad
~ Marathon, Florida Keys ~

6 stone crab claws, cracked with meat removed
1 grapefruit, peeled and sectioned   3 asparagus spears
sprinkle parsley   1 tablespoon virgin olive oil

3 cups iceberg lettuce
3 ripe olives
1 tablespoon balsamic vinegar

Place in a bowl, shredded iceberg lettuce. Add grapefruit sections, stone crab meat and asparagus. Combine olive oil and vinegar. Top with olives and sprinkle with parsley and dressing. Serves 4

Sunshine Citrus Salad
~ Big Pine Key, Florida Keys ~

Salad: 1 orange, sectioned   1 grapefruit, sectioned
1 avocado, sliced or cut in cubes   1 small onion, sliced very thinly and rings separated

Citrus Dressing: 1 teaspoon sugar   1 teaspoon virgin olive oil   3 Key limes, juiced
¼ teaspoon mustard   dash salt

Combine salad ingredients together. Shake citrus dressing well before pouring on top of the salad. Serve chilled.

Virgin Lobster Salad
~ Virgin Islands ~

Lobster Salad: 2 pounds fresh lobster meat, removed from shell   1 small onion, chopped
4 hard boiled eggs, peeled and diced   1 celery stalk, chopped   1 head of lettuce
½ garlic clove   4 green chives, chopped   ½ red bell pepper, chopped
1 tablespoon raisins   ½ yellow bell pepper, chopped   1 cup parmesan cheese
1 tablespoon almonds, chopped

Dressing: 1 tablespoon lime juice   1 teaspoon salt   ½ cup mayonnaise
3 tablespoons sour cream   ½ teaspoon white wine vinegar   ⅛ teaspoon thyme, chopped

Mix all ingredients for the dressing together until light and fluffy. Rub ½ garlic clove over wooden salad bowl. Wash lettuce and shake dry, then place the strips of lettuce in bowl making a bed of lettuce. In a separate bowl, crumble the lobster meat. Add hard boiled eggs, onion, sweet pepper, celery and chives. Mix in the dressing. Sprinkle with almonds, raisins and parmesan cheese. Serve chilled. Serves 4.

Side Dishes

Aros Verde
~ Curaçao ~

2 cups rice, uncooked
3 cups water
dash freshly ground pepper
dash salt

1 cup sweet peas
1 hot pepper, crushed
½ cup parsley, chopped

1 onion, chopped
2 garlic cloves, crushed
1 cup vegetable oil, for frying

In a frying pan, add some oil and fry garlic, onion and hot pepper. Stir in parsley, salt and pepper. Pour in water and bring to a boil. Add in the rice and reduce heat. Cover and cook for 20 minutes or until done. When rice is cooked, add sweet peas. Serves 4.

Arpita di Pampuna
~ Curaçao ~

2 cups pumpkin, boiled, drained and mashed
dash baking powder
vegetable oil, for frying
2 tablespoons sugar

dash salt
1 egg
1 teaspoon cinnamon

½ teaspoon vanilla
½ cup flour
¼ cup milk

Mix all ingredients in blender. Heat some oil on a griddle. Add spoonfuls of mixture on griddle and fry until golden brown. Makes 21 small fritters.

Arroz con Gandules
~ Puerto Rico ~

8 ounces dried pigeon peas
2 tablespoons olive oil
½ green bell pepper, minced

4 teaspoons salt
1 cup sofrito (see page: 22)
4 olives, pitted and chopped

8 cups water
1 teaspoon capers
2 cups rice, well rinsed

Soak dried peas overnight and boil until tender in salted water for 1 hour. Heat oil in frying pan and cook sofrito and bell pepper for 2 minutes. Sauté an additional 4 minutes with capers and olives. Drain cooked peas, saving aside 2½ cups of liquid. Stir in rice and peas and cook on high for 3 minutes. Add saved water and reduce to a moderate heat for and additional 4 minutes or until almost all of the water is absorbed. Simmer and cook until rice is tender, about 20 minutes. Serves 4.

Arroz con Habichuelas
~ Puerto Rico ~

1½ cups dried red kidney beans
3 tablespoons olive oil
1 ounce salt pork, minced
2 teaspoons fresh oregano, diced

2 teaspoons salt
2 teaspoons annatto oil
1 onion, chopped
2 teaspoons tomato paste

5 cups water
2 ounces ham, diced
2 garlic cloves, crushed
2½ cups rice, rinsed well

Soak beans overnight in water. Boil beans in salted water. Reduce heat and simmer for 1 hour or until beans are just soft. Lightly sauté olive oil, annatto oil, onion, garlic, pork, ham and oregano for 5 minutes in a frying pan. Mix in rice and tomato paste. Add the seasoned rice to the beans and cook over medium heat for 4 minutes, until most of the water is absorbed. Cover and simmer for a final 20 minutes, until rice is soft and water is gone. Serves 4-6.

Banana Binja
~ Aruba ~

2 very ripe plantains
3 tablespoons port wine

3 tablespoons dark brown sugar
2 tablespoons water

3 tablespoons butter
dash cinnamon

Peel and cut plantains lengthwise. Melt butter in skillet. Sauté plantains until golden brown on one side. Turn over. In a mixing bowl combine sugar, water, port wine and cinnamon. Pour over plantains. Simmer until liquid thickens. Serve at once. Serves 4.

Berchein na Forno
~ St. Martin ~

2 pounds eggplant, peeled and cut lengthwise into ¼ inch slices
2½ cups coconut cream, fresh or canned, unsweetened
½ teaspoon hot red pepper   ½ pound onions, chopped

1 tablespoon butter
1¼ teaspoon salt
dash freshly ground pepper

Preheat oven to 325°F. Brush butter on the bottom and sides of a baking dish. Place half the eggplant in dish and sprinkle half the onion evenly over the top. Then repeat, making another layer of eggplant and onion. Add black pepper, salt, red pepper and pour in the coconut cream. Cover with foil and bake 45 minutes. Remove foil and brown eggplant for 5-10 minutes. Serves 4.

Bermuda Stuffed Onions
~ Bermuda ~

6 Bermuda onions
⅛ cup almonds, ground
1 teaspoon marjoram, diced
dash salt and freshly ground pepper

4 bouillon cubes
1 cup bread crumbs
1 garlic clove, crushed
¼ teaspoon hot peppers, minced

12 fresh mushrooms
2 tablespoons parsley, diced
4 tablespoons butter
½ teaspoon paprika

Preheat oven to 350°F. Peel onions and slice off tops. Add 2 quarts of water and bouillon in a saucepan, place in onions and bring to a boil. Simmer until just soft, about 30 minutes. Drain and cool. Core the centers of each onion leaving ½ inch thickness of shell. Turn onions upside down to drain. Chop onion centers and mushrooms. Mix in almonds, parsley, garlic, breadcrumbs, marjoram, hot pepper, salt and pepper. Add in 2 tablespoons melted butter. Coat a baking dish with 1 tablespoon of melted butter mixed with paprika. Arrange onions in dish and brush with 1 tablespoon melted butter. Spoon in stuffing and bake for 20 minutes until golden. Serves 6.

Breadfruit Cou Cou
~ Barbados ~

3 tablespoons butter
3 ounces salted meat, minced
freshly ground pepper

1 pound ripe breadfruit, peeled, cored, and cut into 2 inch cubes
water   3 scallions, chopped

Butter the inside of a serving bowl and set aside. Combine meat and breadfruit and cover with 1 inch of water in a large pan. Boil and cook breadfruit until just soft, around 15-20 minutes. Add chopped scallions at the last 5 minutes. Mash well. Add in 3 tablespoons of water and stir. Spoon into prepared serving dish and round top. Indent in the center and top with 1 tablespoon of butter.

Coconut Rice and Peas
~ Jamaica ~

8 ounces kidney beans
2 seeded hot red peppers, minced
2 ounces coconut cream

2 cups long grain rice, rinsed
1 teaspoon thyme, chopped
1 tablespoon melted butter

1 onion, minced
2 garlic cloves, crushed
salt and ground pepper

Place beans in covered pot with water and soak overnight. Cook in large pot with 4 cups of fresh water for 45-60 minutes, until slightly tender. Add in the rest of the ingredients and stir. Add in coconut cream with 1½ cups water. Bring to a boil and cook about 5 minutes, until water is about ½ inch above rice. Cover, reduce heat and simmer an additional 25-30 minutes. Serves 6.

Coo-Coo
~ Grenada ~

14 ounce can coconut milk

1¾ cups coarse cornmeal

vegetable oil, for frying

Papaya Salsa: 1 papaya, peeled and seeded
1 hot pepper, seeded and minced
1 lime, juiced and rind grated

3 tablespoons chopped fresh cilantro
dash freshly ground pepper

½ small red onion, diced

dash salt

Papaya Salsa: Peel papaya, remove seeds and dice. Put in a bowl with hot pepper, onion, cilantro, salt, lime juice and rind. Mix together and set aside. In another pan, pour 2 cups of water, coconut milk and seasoning. Boil and stir in cornmeal with a wooden spoon. Cook for 5 minutes until thick and smooth. Pour onto a flat surface and form a flat 8 inch circle. Allow to cool and firm. Prepare a skillet with heated oil. Brush both sides of coo-coo with oil and fry in pan until each side is golden. Cut into wedgeds and arrange on a serving platter with salsa. Serves 6.

Ducana
~ Antigua ~

5 ounces brown sugar
4 ounces raisins
1½ pound all-purpose flour

2 ounces baking powder
1 cup coconut milk
½ teaspoon nutmeg, freshly grated

1 pound sweet potatoes
2 teaspoon vanilla essence
banana leaf, steamed

Peel and grate potatoes. Add rest of ingredients in a bowl and mix. Cut steamed banana leaf into 10 inch squares pieces. Spoon mixture onto banana squares, fold and tie leaf with string. Poach in lightly salted water. Boil for 1 hour.

Frijoles Negros
~ Antigua ~

1 pound dried black kidney beans
2 garlic cloves, crushed
1 teaspoon cumin

1 tablespoon salt
3 seeded bell green peppers, chopped
¼ cup olive oil

3 medium onions, chopped
3 bay leaves
18 cups water

Sort through beans for debris and rinse well. Put in a large pot with salted water and bring to a boil. Then add all the ingredients and cook for 1 hour, until beans are tender. Simmer for an extra 10 minutes for thickening. Serves 8-10.

Funchi
~ Curaçao ~

1¼ cups chilled water	1½ cups cornmeal	butter
1½ cups room temperature water	2 teaspoons salt	

Mix cornmeal and cool water into a small pan. Butter a serving bowl and set aside. Boil 1½ cups of water with butter and salt in a medium saucepan. After bringing to a boil, turn down to a moderate high heat. Slowly blend in cornmeal batter, stirring constantly. Stir with a wooden spoon until mixture has thickened. The funchi is done when it falls from the sides of the pan easily. Serve hot in prepared bowl.

Island Breeze Coconut and Vegetable Curry
~ Barbados ~

2 sweet potatoes, cubed	1 butternut squash, peeled, and cubed	2 carrots, cubed
3 tablespoons olive oil	3 garlic cloves, crushed	1 onion, chopped
1 hot pepper, seeded and minced	1 teaspoon ground cumin	2 teaspoons curry
2 teaspoons molasses	2 tablespoons tomato purée	2 ounces creamed coconut
dash salt	⅔ cup vegetable broth	
1 lime, juiced and rind grated	1 tablespoon chopped fresh cilantro	

Bring to boil, squash, sweet potatoes and carrots in salted water. Simmer until just soft, about 5-8 minutes. Drain and set aside. Place onion and garlic in a cooking casserole with heated oil and cook until and soft, around 10 minutes. Blend in curry, hot pepper and cumin, and cook for another minute. Add creamed coconut, molasses and tomato purée, cooking an additional minute. Place reserved vegetables, broth, lime juice and rind into cooked blend. Bring to a boil. Then simmer for 10-15 minutes until vegetables are cooked, stirring occasionally. Mix in cilantro. Accompany with white rice. Serves 4.

Kala
~ Curaçao ~

½ pound black-eyed peas	½ teaspoon baking powder	6 tablespoons water
2 teaspoons salt	2 hot peppers	

Soak peas for 1-2 days. Drain, peel and dry well. Then mash the peas and add pepper and salt. Beat with mixer and slowly add water. Consistency should be fluffy. When oil is hot, fry mixture by the spoonful. Makes 25.

Kingston Stuffed Breadfruit
~ Jamaica ~

1 medium breadfruit
dash freshly ground pepper
1 tablespoon salted butter

1 tomato, peeled, seeded, and chopped
dash freshly ground allspice
dash salt

¼ cup heavy cream
1 medium onion, minced

On a grill, roast the breadfruit, allowing to cook for 1 hour. Turn as breadfruit chars. When roasted, cut a circle at the stem and scoop out the heart and discard. Scoop out the breadfruit flesh leaving a ¾ inch thick shell. In a bowl, mix the cream with breadfruit flesh and butter. Next, add seasonings, onion and tomato. Stuff breadfruit mixture into shells, wrap with foil and place in a 300ºF oven for 10 minutes. Unwrap and serve. Serves 6-8.

Mofongo
~ Puerto Rico ~

4 ripe plantains
4 ounces chicharrones (see page: 25)
dash freshly ground black pepper

1 cup vegetable oil, for deep frying
dash salt

½ cup water
2 garlic cloves, crushed

Cut diagonal 1 inch slices of plantains. Soak in water with ½ teaspoon salt for 10 minutes. Drain and reserve water. Fry in hot oil until tender, about 8 minutes. Pat dry on disposable towels. Use a large mortar to grind plantains and chicharrones. Add 2 tablespoons of the reserved water and blend into ground mixture. Add salt, pepper and garlic. Shape into tennis-sized balls. Serve Mofongo hot. Serves 6-8.

Moros Y Cristianos
~ Cuba ~

8 ounces dried black kidney beans
1 onion, minced
dash salt

2 cups water
2 garlic cloves, minced
dash freshly ground black pepper

2 tablespoons olive oil
2 cups rice, well rinsed

Soak beans in a covered pot overnight. Drain and place in a pan with 2 cups of fresh water. Heat to a boil. Simmer beans until just soft, about 20-30 minutes. In a frying pan, heat oil to high and sauté garlic and onion until tender. Add sautéed mixture to beans. Add rice, salt and pepper. Stir over a moderately high heat until water is mostly absorbed. Simmer on low heat until rice is cooked and water is gone, an additional 20 minutes. Serves 6.

Pasta a la Rasta
~ Jamaica ~

4-6 broccoli florets, blanched
1 tablespoon fresh thyme leaves
¼ cup butter
1 bell pepper, chopped
2 teaspoons fresh ginger, minced
½ teaspoon ground allspice
2 cups pumpkin, butternut, or acorn squash, diced
¼ cup corn kernels, fresh, canned, or frozen and thawed

4 ounces uncooked linguine or angel hair pasta
4 mushrooms, chopped
½ small zucchini, chopped
2 garlic cloves, minced
1 chile pepper, seeded and minced
1 teaspoon ground cumin

1 cup water or chicken stock
1 small onion, diced
½ teaspoon salt
1 cup coconut milk
½ teaspoon ground nutmeg
½ teaspoon white pepper
1 teaspoon ground coriander

In a large pot, place pasta and water. Bring to a boil. Cook covered until pasta is tender. Drain pasta and place under cold running water, then set aside. In a medium saucepan melt 2 tablespoons of butter and add ginger, chile pepper, garlic and onion. Sauté for 5 minutes. Pour in water or chicken stock and add in pumpkin. Cook 20 minutes, until pumpkin is tender. Add in thyme, salt, allspice, nutmeg, coconut milk, white pepper, coriander and cumin and simmer for 5 minutes. Place in food processor for 15 seconds or until smooth. Add remaining butter to a large skillet and melt. Add zucchini, bell peppers and mushrooms, sauté for 5 minutes. Add in broccoli and corn and sauté for another 2 minutes. Pour the pumpkin sauce in skillet and stir. Simmer mixture for 1 minute. Add in pasta and mix well. Cook for 2 minutes and serve. Serves 2.

Pigeon Peas and Rice
~ Anguilla ~

2 cups pigeon peas, cooked
2 cups rice
1 sprig thyme

1 onion, chopped
1 teaspoon salt
1 teaspoon hot red pepper, chopped

4 cups water
1 garlic clove, chopped

In a large pot, bring salted water to a boil (for extra flavor substitute water for 2 cups coconut milk). When boiling, add thyme, onion, peppers and garlic. Add rice and cook for 6-8 minutes. Add pigeon peas. Reduce heat to low and cover. Cook until rice is tender. Serves 4.

Riz et Pois Collés
~ Haiti ~

1 ounce salt pork, cut into cubes
½ cup chives, chopped
1 hot pepper, seeded and chopped

1 cup red kidney beans
2 tablespoons vegetable oil
2 cups rice

1 onion, chopped
1 tablespoon butter
1 teaspoon salt

In a large pot, add 4 cups of water and beans. Cook until tender. Drain the beans reserving the water. In a frying pan, fry the salt pork. Add chives, pepper and chopped onion. Put the mixture reserved into water, bring to a boil and add butter. Add the rice and allow to cook for 20 minutes or until rice is done. Serves 4.

Tortilla Clásica Española
~ Cuba ~

5 eggs
1 large onion, thinly sliced

1 pound potatoes, peeled and thinly sliced
dash salt

¾ cup olive oil

Warm oil in a 9 inch skillet. Drop in the potatoes slices individually, keeping them loose. Cook for 15 minutes. Do not brown the potatoes. Add onion and cook until translucent. Drain onions and potatoes, reserving the oil. Wipe skillet clean. In a large mixing bowl, beat eggs and salt. Add potatoes and onions, pushing them to the bottom until completely covered by egg mixture. Let mixture stand and settle for 15 minutes. Heat skillet at high heat with ¼ cup of the reserved oil. Pour mixture, spreading evenly the potatoes and onions. Lower the heat to medium-high. When omelet begins to form, place a plate and flip. Add 2 more tablespoons of oil and place omelet, cooked side up. Cook until omelet is cooked in the center and golden brown on both sides. Serves 4.

Virgin Eggplant
~ Virgin Island ~

3 medium eggplants, cut into cubes and slightly salted
6 tomatoes, peeled and quartered
2 garlic cloves, chopped
½ hot red pepper, chopped
1 tablespoon rum
dash salt
¼ cup parmesan and cheddar cheese, grated

2 large onions
3 green bell peppers, chopped
3 red bell peppers, chopped
½ cup water
dash freshly ground black pepper

1 celery stalk, chopped
1 spring parsley, chopped
2 tablespoons olive oil
1 tablespoon tomato paste
dash oregano
dash thyme

Dry the eggplant and fry in olive oil over medium heat for 8-10 minutes. Place into a baking dish. Preheat to 300°F. In a separate pan, sauté tomato, garlic, celery, onion and peppers for 5 minutes. Add remaining ingredients except rum. Stir until thick, then add rum. Pour sauce over eggplant and cheese. Place in oven and bake until cheese is melted and browned. Serves 6.

Yam Balls
~ Barmuda ~

1 cup dry bread crumbs
1 onion, grated
1 red hot pepper, minced
dash salt

3 pounds yam, peeled
1½ teaspoons parsley, chopped
1 egg
dash freshly ground pepper

¼ hot pepper, chopped
2 sprigs of chives, chopped
½ cup oil

In a steamer, lightly salt yam and cook until soft. Mash with chives, peppers, onion and parsley. Add a dash of salt and pepper. Beat egg and blend well into mashed mixture. Form mixture into 2 inch balls. Roll in breadcrumbs until generously covered. Fry in hot oil until golden brown. Serves 4.

seafood

Ackee and Salt Cod
~ Jamaica ~

8 ounces salt cod
½ teaspoon salt
¼ cup vegetable oil
dash salt

water
1 onion, sliced
1 small hot pepper, seeded and chopped fine
dash ground pepper

2 dozen fresh ackees, ripe
1 tomato, chopped

Soak salt cod overnight in enough water to cover fish. Drain. Remove flesh and toss pods from fresh ackees. Rinse ackee flesh in cold water. Cook ackees with salt in boiling water for around 12 minutes, until tender, yet in whole pieces. Drain and set aside. Place fish in saucepan and cover with water. Boil for around 10 minutes until soft in texture. Remove bones and skin, then flake the fish apart. Heat oil over moderate heat in a separate saucepan. Add onion and hot pepper. Sauté until onion is translucent. Add tomato and fish. Stir together for about 3-4 minutes. Add ackees, salt and pepper to taste. Cook, stirring occasionally for 5 minutes. Serves 6.

Atlantic Ginger Crayfish
~ Dominica ~

1 teaspoon black peppercorns
dash salt
12 crayfish, cleaned, washed in lime, left in shell

1 tablespoon ginger, grated
1 lime, juiced

3 garlic cloves, grated
2 ounces butter

Rub salt into crayfish. In a wok, heat butter on low until frothy. Add crayfish and fry until crispy. Add garlic, ginger and peppercorns. Add in the lime juice and remove from heat. Serve with yellow saffron rice or annatto rice which has been boiled with a stick of cinnamon. Serves 2.

Balchi di Pisca (Fish Balls)
~ Aruba ~

1 salted cod or bakijow (about 1 pound)
1 tomato, peeled and chopped
½ teaspoon red hot pepper sauce
dash freshly ground pepper
dash salt

3 medium potatoes, peeled and diced
½ green bell pepper, chopped
1 medium onion, peeled and chopped

1 garlic clove, minced
dash nutmeg
1 egg, beaten

Soak cod in water for 24 hours. Discard water. In a saucepan, place cod in fresh water. Simmer gently until fish flakes easily with a fork. Strain and reserve a small amount of broth. Debone cod and set aside. Fill a saucepan with water and bring to a boil. Add potatoes. Drain water when potatoes are tender. Mash cod and potatoes. In blender or food processor, combine tomato, green pepper, onion, garlic, red hot pepper sauce, nutmeg, salt and pepper. Blend for a few seconds, then pour over mashed fish mixture. Combine well and add egg to mixture. If mixture is too dry, add reserved stock 1 tablespoon at a time until moist enough to mold. Mold mixture into 1 inch balls and fry in deep oil until golden brown. Serves 6.

Beach Lover's Red Snapper
~ U.S. Virgin Islands ~

6 small red snappers, cleaned ready for cooking
2 medium tomatoes, peeled, seeded and chopped
2 teaspoons hot pepper, minced
1 whole chile
½ cup vegetable oil for frying
dash freshly ground black pepper

½ cup flour
2 limes, juiced
2 springs fresh thyme, or ½ teaspoon dried

3 cups water
½ cup cider vinegar
1½ tablespoons salt
1 medium onion, minced

Wash fish in a mixture of salted water and vinegar. Score the fish diagonally from head to tail. In a bowl, mix minced chile, pepper and salt together, forming a paste. Place a small amount into the slits in the fish. Pour lime juice all over fish and let sit for at least 1 hour. Remove fish and dry it off. Roll fish in flour and shake off excess. In a large skillet, heat oil and add fish. Fry on medium heat until golden brown. Remove fish and set aside. To the same oil, add thyme, onion, salt, pepper and whole chile. Cook until onion is light brown. Add in tomato and cook until the mixture becomes a thick sauce. Add water and bring sauce to a boil. Reduce heat to low and cook another 5 minutes. Add in fish and cook 5 more minutes, turning the fish once. Before serving, add a squeeze of lime juice and stir. Serve with rice and peas. Serves 6.

Bermuda Fish Cakes
~ Bermuda ~

1 pound codfish, deboned
1 dash thyme
2 sprigs chives, diced
dash salt

sprig parsley, finely chopped
1 large onion, diced
¼ teaspoon hot pepper, minced
dash freshly ground pepper

6 potatoes, peeled
1 garlic clove, crushed
2 eggs, beaten
vegetable oil, for frying

Soak codfish in water overnight. Drain and put in a pot with potatoes, pour in enough water to cover. Add thyme, parsley and onion into the water. Boil together for an hour. Using a large sieve to catch seasoning, drain off cooking water. Reserve seasoning and put the codfish in one bowl and the potatoes in another. Mash each one separately and then combine. Mix in all the remaining ingredients except the eggs, salt and pepper. Fold in eggs and season with salt and pepper. Fill a pan half way with vegetable oil and heat. Using a spoon, scoop up the mix and roll into a ball. Then roll in a light coating of flour and deep fry until golden and crispy. Drain and serve. Makes 2 dozen.

Buccaneer Crawfish with Rice
~ Bahamas ~

2 crawfish, peeled and cut into bite-size pieces
1 pound rice
1 celery stalk, minced
2 ounces tomato paste
1 sprig thyme, minced
dash salt

2 medium green bell peppers, minced
2 tablespoons vegetable oil
2 garlic cloves, minced
1 sprig chive, minced
dash freshly ground pepper

1 ounce pork fat, minced
2 onions, minced
1 can pigeon peas
4 cups water
vegetable oil, for frying

In a skillet, fry the pork fat, onion, celery and green pepper in vegetable oil. Add crawfish, tomato paste, peas and water. When mixture comes to a boil, add remaining ingredients. Cover and cook for 20 minutes. Serve while hot. Serves 8.

Calypso Shrimp Créole
~ Caribbean ~

1 onion, minced
3 tablespoons butter
2 chives, minced
1 green bell pepper, minced
1 teaspoon fresh ginger, minced

3 pounds raw shrimp, shelled and deveined
3 tomatoes, peeled, seeded and chopped
1 scallion, including the green top, minced
2 branches fresh thyme or ½ teaspoon dried
2 teaspoons hot pepper

1 garlic clove, minced

In a large frying pan, heat butter. Add green pepper, garlic, thyme, ginger, onion, scallion and chives. Sauté until onion is browned. Add shrimp, chile and tomatoes, then cover. Cook on medium heat for 15 minutes, stirring occasionally and adding water if sauce becomes too dry. Serve with white rice. Serves 6.

Camarones Enchilados
~ Cuba ~

1 pound peeled shrimp
1 onion, minced
½ teaspoon fresh oregano, chopped
½ teaspoon cumin
dash freshly ground black pepper

1 lime, juiced
3 garlic cloves, crushed
2 teaspoons white wine vinegar
½ cup water
2 tablespoons fresh parsley, chopped fine

2 tablespoons olive oil
¼ cup tomato purée
1 bay leaf
1 teaspoon salt

Squeeze fresh lime juice over shrimp and rub in. Place large frying pan over moderate heat with oil and fry onion for one minute. Add in garlic, parsley and oregano. Fry for another minute. Stir in tomato paste. Cook for 5 minutes. Add all remaining ingredients and gently simmer until shrimp are completely cooked, about 10-15 minutes. Serve immediately. Serves 6.

Caribbean Calamari Créole
~ Aruba ~

4 whole calamari, cleaned
1 tablespoon olive oil
¼ yellow bell pepper
1 tablespoon basil, chopped
1 tablespoon capers

1 garlic clove
¼ red bell pepper
1 tablespoon celery, chopped
½ small can tomato paste
dash freshly ground pepper

1 small onion
¼ green bell pepper
½ hot pepper, seeded
1 tomato, sliced into wedges
dash salt

In a pan with hot oil, sauté peppers and onion. Add in calamari, then capers and tomato paste, mix well. Add celery, tomato wedges, garlic, basil, salt and pepper. Cook for 4 minutes. Garnish with pieces of callaloo bush, slice of lemon, and guava slices. Serves 4.

Caribbean Sea Red Snapper
~ Aruba ~

2 pounds red snapper fillets
3 garlic cloves, minced
1 large onion, chopped
dash freshly ground pepper

½ cup lime juice
4 tablespoons butter
1 green bell pepper, chopped
2 large tomatoes, peeled and chopped

3 scallions, finely chopped
1 cup flour
dash salt and

Make a marinade of lime juice, scallions, 1 garlic clove, salt and pepper. Pour over fish and refrigerate for one hour. In a skillet, melt butter. Coat fish with flour and fry until golden brown. In the skillet with fish drippings, sauté onion, bell pepper and 2 garlic cloves. Add tomatoes and simmer for twenty minutes. When sauce thickens, place fish in skillet and heat thoroughly. Serves 4.

Coconut Conch
~ Key West ~

1 conch, skin peeled off
dash curry
1 tablespoon butter

1cup fresh coconut milk
1 sprig parsley

1 onion
1 sprig chives

Slice conch into 1 inch pieces. Add butter to a pan and all seasonings except curry. Bring to a quick simmer. Add conch and sauté until light brown. Slowly add coconut milk to pan. Add a dash of curry and simmer 10 minutes before serving. Serves 1.

Crab and Shrimp Pilau
~ St. Vincent ~

½ pound crabmeat
1 medium onion, minced
3 garlic cloves, minced
1½ cups rice, uncooked
1 tomato, diced
2 tablespoons curry powder

20 large shrimp, peeled and deveined
1 cup pigeon peas or kidney beans, cooked
3½ cups coconut milk, fresh or unsweetened, canned
1 Scotch Bonnet Pepper, seeded and minced
dash freshly ground black pepper
¼ cup butter, melted   dash salt

In saucepan, place butter, Scotch Bonnet Pepper, garlic, tomato and onion and sauté for 7 minutes. Add salt, black pepper and curry powder, then sauté another 2 minutes. Stir in rice and coat with curry mixture cook for 2 minutes. Pour in coconut milk and cook for 20 minutes on low heat. Add in pigeon peas, crabmeat and shrimp. Cook for 10 minutes, or until rice absorbs all the liquid and shrimp is pink and firm. Stir occasionally. Serve with warm bread. Serves 4.

Crabby Cakes
~ Key Largo, Florida ~

1 pound crabmeat, shelled
¼ cup milk
2 tablespoons scallions, chopped
dash Worcestershire sauce
1 lime, cut into wedges

¾ cup seasoned bread crumbs
¼ cup chopped fresh parsley
3 tablespoons butter
dash salt
2 cups tartar sauce

3 eggs
2 tablespoons lime juice
2 garlic cloves, crushed
dash pepper

Drain crabmeat. Combine crabmeat with all ingredients except the butter, lime wedges and garlic. In a large skillet, heat butter and add garlic. Shape crab mixture into 2 inch patties. Sauté 4 minutes on each side until golden brown. Drain on paper towels. Serve with lime wedges and tartar sauce. Serves 8.

———————————

Crabmeat Omelet
~ Puerto Rico ~

10 eggs
1 tablespoon fresh parsley

¼ pound Jueyes (Land Crab), shelled
1 tablespoon butter

1 tablespoon chives

Shell and drain the crabmeat and set aside. Separate the eggs. Beat the egg yolks in a bowl. Beat egg white in another bowl until fluffy. Fold in crabmeat into the egg white and fold in egg yolks. In a skillet melt butter. Add mixture and cook until brown on the bottom. Fold omelet over in half and serve. Serves 4.

———————————

Crawfish Bahama-Mama
~ Bahamas ~

6 large crawfish tails, shelled
1 tablespoon fresh parsley

4 fresh garlic cloves, chopped
1 lime, cut in wedges

⅓ cup melted butter
dash paprika

Shell crawfish tails and reserve meat. Slice meat at diagonal in the shape of a tail. Sauté garlic in butter until lightly brown. Add crawfish slices. Cook at high heat for 4 minutes or until crawfish is done. Do not over cook. In a serving dish arrange pieces in the shape of tails. Drizzle with garlic butter. Garnish with parsley and lime wedges dusted with paprika. Serves 6.

———————————

Curry Cascadura
~ Trinidad ~

10 cascadura or shrimps
½ teaspoon ground cloves
1½ cup water
2 tablespoons fresh chives, minced

2 onions, chopped
4 tomatoes, peeled, seeded and chopped
5 tablespoons curry powder
dash freshly ground black pepper

3 tablespoons coconut oil
1 lime, juiced
dash salt

Wash cascadura thoroughly with lime juice and salt. Rinse with water and season with salt, pepper, cloves and chives. In a large skillet, heat oil on medium heat. Add curry powder and stir. When curry powder is about to scorch, add cascadura and cook 10 minutes, turning fish from time to time. Add onions and tomatoes and brown. Lower heat and cook for 25 minutes. Serve with white rice.

Famous Curried Fish with Green Mangoes
~ Trinidad ~

2 pounds fish filets	2 teaspoons lemon juice	3 tablespoons olive oil
1 onion, minced	3 garlic cloves, crushed	1½ tablespoons curry powder
1 teaspoon cumin	1 hot pepper, seeded and minced	1 tomato, chopped
¼ cup water	2 green mangoes, peeled, seeded and sliced	
dash salt	dash freshly ground black pepper	

Sprinkle lemon juice over fish. Heat oil in a large saucepan over medium heat. Sauté onion and garlic. Add spices and stir occasionally for 3 minutes. Add tomato, mangoes and hot pepper. Cook for an additional 3 minutes. Add fish fillets, water, salt and pepper into sauté mixture. Reduce heat and simmer for 10 minutes or until fish is fully cooked. Serve hot. Serves 6.

Fish Fillets in Coconut
~ Dominican Republic ~

4 large snapper fillets	½ teaspoon dried oregano	1 lime
1 chopped onion	1 tablespoon olive oil	1 bay leaf
4 cloves or chopped garlic	1 teaspoon tomato paste	1 chopped celery stalk
1 can unsweetened coconut milk	1 tomato, chopped, seeded and blanched	½ cup parsley
½ cup pineapple juice	½ cup oregano	dash salt and ground pepper

Wash fish and pat dry. Pour lime juice over fillets, then sprinkle on oregano, pepper and salt. Cover and refrigerate over night. In a pan, sauté garlic, celery, onion and tomato in oil for 1 minute. Add pineapple juice, bay leaf, coconut milk and tomato paste. Simmer for about 10 minutes. In another pan, brown the fish on both sides. Pour sauce over fish and simmer for 5 minutes, turning fillets over once halfway through cooking. Sprinkle with parsley and oregano. Serves 4.

Fisherman's Special Baked Grouper
~ Florida Keys ~

4 grouper filets	dash freshly ground black pepper	dash red pepper flakes
2 tablespoons lemon juice	dash salt	½ onion, diced
½ green bell pepper, diced	½ tomato, diced	

Season fish with black pepper, salt and red pepper. Drizzle lemon juice over filets and place on a baking dish. Add onion, green pepper and tomato on top of filets. Preheat oven to 300°F and bake fish for 20 minutes. Serves 4.

Fisherman's Special Grill Swordfish
~ Florida Keys ~

6 swordfish steaks, cut 1 inch thick   dash salt and freshly ground pepper   mayonnaise

Preheat barbeque grill. Season both sides of fish with salt and pepper. Spread bountiful amounts of mayonnaise on each side. Grill about 5 minutes. Serves 6.

———————————

Fort-de-France Blaff
~ Martinique ~

4 small red snappers, scaled and cleaned with heads

6 limes, juiced

3 garlic cloves, crushed

1 bouquet garni (bundle of spices)

1 hot pepper, pricked with a fork

1 onion, sliced

1 sprig fresh thyme, or ¼ teaspoon dried

1 sprig fresh parsley

 dash freshly ground black pepper

6 allspice berries, crushed

1½ quarts water

2 chives

dash salt

In a large bowl, add half the lime juice, half the allspice, half the chile, half the garlic clove and half the salt and pepper, mix well. Add fish to the marinade and set aside for 1 hour. Place all remaining ingredients except half the lime juice and fish in a pot and bring to a boil. When water is at a rolling boil, place fish in the liquid and boil. (Listen to the blaff!). Remove fish and serve with their cooking liquid and remaining lime juice. Serve with rice. Serves 4.

———————————

Fricassée de Langouste
~ Nevis ~

1½-2 pounds lobster, quartered

1 onion, chopped

1 whole hot pepper

2 teaspoons fresh parsley, chopped

⅓ cup white wine vinegar

½ lime, juiced

4 green onions

1 teaspoon fresh thyme, chopped

1 tablespoon tomato purée

dash salt and freshly ground pepper

2 tablespoons olive oil

2 garlic cloves, crushed

dash ground allspice

1 bay leaf

2 tablespoons water

Sprinkle lobster with lime juice. Heat oil in a pan and sauté the lobster until it turns pink, about 3-5 minutes. Add onions, 1 garlic clove, hot pepper and spices. Simmer with wine and remaining ingredients, cooking slowly until lobster is white and soft, approximately 10-15 minutes. Before serving add remaining garlic. Serves 4.

———————————

Fried Fish
~ Barbados ~

6 fish pieces, cleaned

½ teaspoon ground, fresh ginger

1 teaspoon dried parsley

½ cup cold water

1 lime, juiced

2½ tablespoons all-purpose flour

½ teaspoon garlic, onion and celery salt

½ teaspoon ground, fresh black pepper

½ teaspoon dried thyme

½ cup vegetable oil

Sprinkle lime juice on fish. Season with celery salt, ginger, pepper, thyme and parsley. Let stand for a minimum of 10 minutes. Mix flour and water to form a thin, smooth batter. Coat fish on all sides. Heat oil on medium high heat in a shallow frying pan. Fry several pieces of fish at a time until golden brown on both sides. Serve hot after draining well on paper towels. Serves 6.

Frizzle Salt Cod
~ Barbados ~

8 ounces salt cod
¼ teaspoon white pepper
¼ - ½ cup olive oil

1 onion, minced
2 sprigs fresh thyme
parsley, chopped for garnish

2 scallions, chopped
1 garlic clove, crushed

Soak salt cod in water for at least 4 hours or overnight. Drain. Put fish in medium saucepan and add water to cover fish. After bringing to a boil, simmer for 10-15 minutes or until soft. Flake very finely. Mix chopped vegetables and spices in a small bowl. Bring oil to a high heat in saucepan and stir in all ingredients. Cook until golden brown. Garnish with fresh parsley.

Garlic Lemon Tilapia
~ Jamaica ~

3 pounds tilapia fillets
¼ cup fresh parsley, chopped
1 cup mayonnaise

4 teaspoons lime juice
½ cup grated parmesan cheese
½ cup yellow, red and green bell peppers

6 teaspoons butter, melted
2 garlic cloves, chopped

Rinse and drain the tilapia fillets. Place fish in a broiler pan and top with half of the lime juice and half of the melted butter. Place pan in oven (or broiler) ¾ inch from source of heat. Cook for 5 minutes. Add garlic, parsley, mayonnaise, remaining butter and the other half of the lime juice in a separate bowl and mix together. Remove tilapia from broiler, add mayonnaise mixture and sprinkle with parmesan cheese. Broil for 2 more minutes until sauce puffs and turns brown. Remove from broiler and place on a serving dish. Garnish with bell peppers. Serve with rice or pasta.

Ginger Marinated Tuna
~ Cayman Islands ~

4 tuna steaks, ¾ inch thick

Marinade: 1 onion, minced
3 tablespoons ginger, grated

4 scallions, minced
½ teaspoon hot pepper sauce

2 garlic cloves, crushed
dash salt

Cucumber Salad: 1 cucumber, peeled, seeded and chopped
1 garlic clove, crushed

1 hot pepper, seeded and minced

dash salt
1 tablespoon fresh lime juice

Place tuna steaks in a shallow dish. Blend all the marinade ingredients together and pour over fish, making sure steaks are thoroughly bathed in sauce. Cover and soak for 2 hours in the refrigerator.

Cucumber Salad: Salt cucumber and set aside for 10 minutes. Pat dry. Mix cucumber, lime and chili in a bowl.

Preheat the broiler. Broil for 5-7 minutes on each side and serve with fresh cucumber salad. Serves 4.

Green Turtle Stew
~ Cayman Islands ~

2 pounds turtle meat
1 can (16 ounces) peeled tomatoes
1 cup red wine
1½ teaspoons browning
vegetable oil

4 onions, chopped
4 sprigs chives, minced
½ hot pepper, seeded and chopped
dash freshly ground pepper
4 medium limes, juiced

6 ripe tomatoes, chopped
2 garlic cloves, minced
1½ cups water
dash salt

Wash turtle meat with lime juice and water. Season with onion, tomato, chives, garlic and wine. Marinate overnight in refrigerator. In a large pot, add a little oil. Remove chives, garlic and onions and fry them in a pot. Add the turtle meat and fry for about 15 minutes. Add browning and hot pepper. Simmer on stove for about 2 hours. Add pepper and salt to taste. Serve hot over white rice. Serves 4.

Harinas con Jaibas
~ Cuba ~

⅔ cup olive oil
1 green bell pepper, chopped
2 tablespoons vinegar
4 cups coarse yellow cornmeal

10 small crabs (or about 5 pounds)
6 garlic cloves, minced
dash freshly ground pepper
dash salt

3 onions, chopped
1½ cups tomato purée
5 quarts water

Wash crabs thoroughly, then crack each shell with a mallet. Remove crab meat from shells. Heat oil in a large pot and sauté onions and green pepper. Add garlic and cook for 2 minutes. Stir in tomato purée and vinegar, cook for an additional 2 minutes. Add the remaining ingredients except for the crabs and bring to a boil. Stir constantly to avoid lumps in cornmeal. When cornmeal thickens, lower the heat and add crabs. Cover and simmer for 1 hour, stirring occasionally. Serves 8.

Hemingway's Great Dish
~ Cuba ~

13 pounds lobster tail
¼ cup mushrooms, sliced, cooked
2 broccoli tops, cooked
1 teaspoon capers
½ cup béchamel sauce

½ pound fish fillet
4 large carrots, cooked
2 pieces asparagus, cooked
1 tablespoon vegetable oil

1 pound jumbo shrimp
1 large ripe tomato
1 tablespoon olive oil
½ cup alcaparra sauce

Peel shells from lobster tails. Pour a little oil over lobster, fish and shrimp, then season with salt and pepper. Place shrimp, lobster and fish on a grill and cook for 1 minute on each side. Cut off the top of the tomato, remove all seeds and stuff with alcaparra sauce, olive oil and béchamel sauce. Place tomato in the center of a large plate, arranging the shellfish, fish and vegetables around the plate. Sprinkle the capers over the dish. Serves 2.

Holiday Ginger Broiled Tuna
~ Islamorada, Florida Keys ~

4 tuna steaks, ¾ inch thick

Marinade: 4 scallions, chopped   *1 small onion, finely chopped*   *2 garlic cloves, crushed*
1 inch piece fresh root ginger, grated   *½ teaspoon hot pepper sauce*   *dash salt*

In a shallow dish, mix scallions, onion, garlic, ginger and hot pepper sauce. Salt and pepper to taste. Place tuna steaks in dish and coat with marinade. Cover and refrigerate for 2 hours. Broil tuna for 5-7 minutes on each side. Serves 4.

_____

Kerri Kerri
~ Aruba ~

2 pounds fish (wahoo, baby shark or king fish)   *2 garlic cloves, chopped*
1 teaspoon annatto seeds   *2 tablespoons cumin*   *1 tablespoon olive oil*
1 sprig Aruban basil, chopped   *1 large onion, chopped*

Cook the fish and remove bones. Shred the fish. In a pan, cook annatto seeds in oil until a dark golded brown. Add garlic and onion to the annatto oil and sauté. Next, add in salt, basil and cumin. Add the shredded fish and simmer. Serves 4.

_____

Key Lime-Mango-Coconut Shrimp Kabobs
~ Key West, Florida Keys ~

1 pound shrimp, shelled, deveined and rinsed   *3 cups canola oil*
2 eggs, beaten   *milk*

Batter: 1 cup white bread crumbs   *1 cup grated, sweetened coconut flakes*

Dip: 1 tablespoon Key lime juice   *1 cup ripe mango, peeled and puréed*   *8 ounces lemon yogurt*

Combine dip ingredients and refrigerate. In a bowl, soak shrimp for 20 minutes with sufficient milk to cover them. Mix coconut flakes and breadcrumbs in a shallow dish. Dip shrimp in egg, coat with batter and drop in hot oil. Fry until golden brown. Drain on paper. Arrange shrimp in a bowl with the dip in the center and long toothpicks. Fills a 12 inch serving platter.

Langostas Enchiladas
~ Cuba ~

3 pounds lobster tails
1 green bell pepper, chopped
dash salt
¾ cup dry white wine
½ cup parsley, chopped

½ cup olive oil
3 garlic cloves, minced
dash freshly ground pepper
2 tablespoons white vinegar

1 large onion, chopped
1 cup tomato sauce
dash sugar
1 bay leaf

Cut the lobster tails and divide them at each joint. Remove the vein by inserting a toothpick through center of each section. In a large saucepan, heat oil and sauté lobster tails until shells turn red. Add onion and green pepper and sauté for 3 minutes. Add remaining ingredients, cover and sauté for 30 minutes. Remove bay leaf and serve. Serves 6.

Lobster Paella
~ Cuba ~

2 live lobsters, 1½ pounds each
½ teaspoon black pepper
1 pound chicken thighs, skinless, boneless and chopped
1 medium bell pepper, seeded and diced
1 tomato, diced
1 teaspoon saffron threads
3½ cups lobster or chicken stock

1 cup green peas, frozen and thawed
2 tablespoons butter, melted

2 cups rice, uncooked
1 medium onion, diced
1 jalapeño pepper, seeded, and minced

12 cups water
½ teaspoon salt
1 teaspoon paprika
½ pound chorizo
2 cloves garlic, minced
½ cup dry white wine

Bring water to a boil and add lobsters. Cook 12 minutes then drain. Reserve water for stock if desired. Cool lobster by running under cold water. Remove all the meat from lobster and set aside. In a large saucepan, add butter and chicken and sauté over medium heat, cooking for 10 minutes. Remove chicken with slotted spoon and keep warm. In the same pan add chorizo to juices and cook 5 minutes. Add jalapeño pepper, onion, garlic, tomato and bell pepper and sauté for 10 minutes until vegetables are soft. Add in lobster stock, rice, seasonings and wine. Cover and simmer for 15 minutes, stirring frequently. Add in peas, lobster meat and chicken. Cook until liquid is absorbed. Serve paella with warm bread. Add Sofrito (see page 22) or Créole sauce over top for an extra taste. Serves 6-8.

Lobster Patties
~ Cayman Islands ~

2 pounds lobster meat, well ground
1 hot pepper, seeded and minced
2 cups potatoes, boiled and mashed
dash freshly ground pepper
2 cups all-purpose flour with a dash of salt

3 garlic cloves, crushed
2 stalks celery, minced
1 sprig chives, minced
1 cup fresh parsley, chopped

1 onion, minced
2 eggs, beaten
vegetable oil
dash salt

Knead together lobster, onion, garlic, hot pepper, celery and mashed potatoes. Fold flour and eggs into lobster mixture. Add salt and pepper. Mix in the remainder of the ingredients and shape into 2 inch balls. Roll in seasoned flour and flatten into patties. Fry until golden brown. Serves 4.

Lobster Thermidor
~ Virgin Islands ~

2 fresh lobsters, 1½ pounds each	1 egg yolk, beaten	2 tablespoons salt
1 lime	1 tablespoon flour	1 tablespoon butter
¼ cup milk	½ teaspoon French mustard	½ red bell pepper, chopped
½ green bell pepper, chopped	1 onion, peeled and grated	¼ cup lobster stock
1 tablespoon rum	3 tablespoons parmesan cheese	½ cup heavy cream

Preheat oven to 350°F. Bring a large pot with salted water to a boil. Place lobsters into water head in first and boil for 3 minutes. Remove and cut lengthwise. Reserve water as stock. Clean out entrails and wash with water and fresh lime. Put lobster on a lightly greased baking sheet. Bake for 12 minutes or until lobster meat begins to come off the shell, about 12 minutes. Do not overcook. In a frying pan, melt butter and sauté peppers and onion until soft. Stir in flour to make a smooth paste. Slowly add lobster stock (water from the pot the lobsters were boiled) and milk. Stir until paste is smooth and free from lumps. When creamy, add mustard and rum, remove from heat and let cool. Remove lobster from shells and cut into 3-4 slices each. Place lobster meat back into shells. Mix egg yolks, cheese and heavy cream into the cooled sauce. Simmer 2 minutes over low heat. Spoon mixture into the lobster shells. Bake or broil until lightly browned. Serve hot. Serves 4.

Mallory Market Mahi-Mahi
~ Key West ~

Tamarind Tartar Sauce: 2 tablespoons lime juice   ¼ cup tamarind juice
1 tablespoon onion, grated   ¼ cup green and black olives, chopped   1 cup mayonnaise

Fufu: 6 ounces bacon, about 6 slices, diced   1 onion, chopped
3 ripened plantains, peeled and cut into 1 inch cubes

Plantain Crust: 4 cups vegetable oil, for frying   4 eggs, beaten
6 mahi-mahi fillets, 7-8 ounces each (halibut may be substituted)   dash salt
4 green plantains, peeled and sliced   1 cup all-purpose flour   dash freshly ground pepper

For the tartar sauce, combine all ingredients and refrigerate. Fufu is prepared by frying bacon bits until crispy, then adding in sautéed onion and garlic. Place ripened plantains into boiling water and cook on simmer until just soft. Drain off water and mash well. Stir in bacon bits mixture to create fufu. Fry the sliced green plantains until golden, about 3-4 minutes. Drain on paper towels and cool. When crisp, grind plantain slices in a food processor. Pour out onto a plate. Prepare two bowls, one with flour and the other with beaten eggs. Season mahi-mahi on both sides. Coat with egg on only one side. Slide egged side across flour. Coat floured side with green plantain mixture to finalize coating. In a clean skillet, fry the mahi-mahi coated side first in fresh oil. Fry until golden, 4-5 minutes each side. On serving plates, mound the fufu in center. Place crusted fish on top of the fufu and top with tamarind tartar. Serves 6.

Mango Glazed Lobster
~ Key Largo, Florida Keys ~

4 (6 ounce) Florida lobster tails, split lengthwise
¼ teaspoon fresh ground pepper
2 teaspoons virgin olive oil
1 teaspoon unsalted butter
1 teaspoon salt

Mango Glaze: 1 very ripe mango, peeled, cut from the pit and puréed
½ cup red wine vinegar
3 tablespoons packed brown sugar
1 teaspoon minced fresh ginger
1 teaspoon minced jalapeño pepper
1 teaspoon virgin olive oil
dash salt and ground pepper
1 teaspoon fresh ginger

For mango gaze, combine all ingredients and mix well. Preheat oven to 350°F. Season Florida lobster tails with salt and pepper. Heat oil in a heavy skillet over medium heat. Add butter and cook lobster tails, flesh side down for 2-3 minutes, or until the flesh turns to white. Turn and brush the mango glaze on the meat. Roast in the oven for 7-8 minutes, until the flesh is opaque. Serves 4.

Mango Style Grouper
~ Islamorada, Florida Keys ~

6 apples, peeled and sliced
1 lime, juiced
3 avocados, peeled and sliced
3 pounds grouper fillets, 1 inch thick
4 ripe mangoes, peeled and sliced into strips
sesame oil
3 oranges, juiced
½ pound baby spinach

Seasoning Mixture: 6 tablespoons onion, minced
2 tablespoons ground allspice
4 teaspoons ground thyme
½ teaspoon hot peppers, chopped
1 avocado, peeled and sliced, for garnish
2 tablespoons brown sugar
4 teaspoons ground cinnamon
1 tablespoon blackened seasoning
6 tablespoons garlic, minced
2 tablespoons ground paprika
1½ teaspoons ground nutmeg

Burn charcoal in grill down to embers. Crush all ingredients for seasoning mixture with a mortar and pestle. Rub mixture on both sides of the fish fillets. Let marinate for about 30 minutes. Grill fish until outside is well done, but inside is still tender. Remove fish from grill and keep warm. In a bowl, add mangoes and apples. Rub fruit with sesame oil and grill for about 1 minute. Toss fruit and fish in a large bowl with lime and orange juices. Serve on a bed of steamed baby spinach. Top with avocado slices. Serves 6.

Matété Crabs
~ Martinique ~

6 live (1 pound) crabs
2 tablespoons unsalted butter
2 tablespoons light olive oil
1 lime, juiced
1 onion, minced
1 scallion, including top, minced
3 cups cooked rice
1 garlic clove, sliced
1 branch fresh thyme, minced
¾ cup boiling water
dash black pepper
1 hot pepper, seeded and minced
3 quarts water
1 bay leaf
3 chives, minced
1 sprig parsley, minced
dash salt

In a saucepan, bring water to a boil. Add live crabs to water and cook for 10 minutes. Drain crabs and cut into small pieces, removing broken shells. Heat oil and butter in a skillet. Add chives, garlic, onion, thyme, scallion, parsley and crab meat. Cook for 10 minutes. Moisten the mixture with ¾ cup boiling water. Add salt, pepper, bay leaf, chile and lime juice. Cook over low heat for 20 minutes or until mixture forms a thick sauce. Be careful of possible crab shell bits. Serve with rice. Serves 6.

Octopus Créole
~ Guadeloupe ~

1 pound octopus meat	3 garlic cloves, chopped	1 sprig parsley, chopped
3 coriander leaves, chopped	2 onions, chopped	1 sprig thyme, chopped
4 sprigs chives, chopped	3 oregano leaves, chopped	½ orange bell pepper
½ red bell pepper	½ green bell pepper	1 can peeled tomatoes
½ teaspoon hot peppers, chopped	1 tablespoon rum	pinch cumin
1 tablespoon butter	1 teaspoon lime juice	dash salt and ground pepper

In a large iron pot, melt butter over medium heat. Reduce heat and add octopus. Cook until brown. Add garlic and onions and simmer until tender. Add remaining ingredients except salt, pepper and rum. Simmer for 5 minutes. Add in salt, pepper and rum. Simmer until octopus is soft. If sauce is too thick add water. Serve with white rice. Serves 4.

Oyster Stuffed Sea Bass
~ Puerto Rico ~

1 cup breadcrumbs	3 pounds sea bass, cleaned, scaled with head and tail attached	
½ teaspoon dried oregano	1 pint raw oysters, drained and coarsely chopped	
dash salt and freshly ground pepper	1 garlic clove, peeled and minced	dash tarragon
¼ cup melted butter	1 tablespoon vinegar	4 bacon strips

Preheat oven to 370°F. Rinse fish and pat dry. In a bowl, combine breadcrumbs, oysters, salt, pepper, oregano, garlic, tarragon, butter and vinegar. Make 4 vertical slits on one side of fish. Fill the slits with the stuffing. Close the slits with wooden toothpicks. In a large baking dish, arrange fish with slit side up. Place bacon slices on top of fish. Bake and baste frequently for 30 minutes. Remove toothpicks before serving. Serves 4.

Paella de Langosta
~ Key West ~

2 live lobsters, 2 pounds each	1 pound skinless, boneless chopped chicken thighs	
½ pound chorizo	6 fresh or frozen squid, cleaned and cut into thin rings	
1 jalapeño pepper, seeded and minced	1 medium bell pepper, seeded and diced	
3½ cups lobster or chicken stock	2 cups Valencia (short-grain) uncooked rice	
2 tablespoons melted butter	1 medium onion, diced	1 tomato, diced
1 teaspoon paprika	½ cup dry white wine	1 teaspoon saffron threads
½ teaspoon salt	½ teaspoon freshly ground pepper	1 bay leaf
1 cup green peas, frozen and thawed	12 cups water	2 garlic cloves, minced

Boil lobsters for 12 minutes and drain. Remove the meat from lobster and set aside. Place butter and chicken in a large saucepan and sauté over medium heat for 10 minutes. With a slotted spoon, remove the chicken and keep warm. Cook chorizo with the pan juices for 5 minutes. Add onion, bell pepper, tomato and garlic and sauté for 10 minutes. Add rice, lobster stock, wine and seasonings and cover. Simmer for 15 minutes, stirring occasionally. Add the lobster meat, chicken and peas and cook until all the liquid is absorbed. Makes 8 servings.

Pisquettes
~ Haiti ~

1 pound whitebait
1 lemon, juiced
dash salt

½ cup flour
vegetable oil, for frying
dash freshly ground black pepper

¼ teaspoon poultry seasoning

On a heavy skillet, heat 3 inches of oil to 375ºF. Wash fish in lemon juice and dry. Put seasonings and flour in a brown paper bag. Add the fish and shake until coated with the mixture. Fry the fish in the hot oil for 3-5 minutes until they are crispy. Place on paper towels and drain. Serves 1.

Poisson Grillé
~ Martinique ~

1½-2 pound red snapper or any white-fleshed fish

Marinade: 1 onion, sliced
2 limes, juiced
dash salt

2 garlic cloves, crushed
1 hot red pepper, crushed, and seeded
dash freshly ground black pepper

¼ teaspoon ground allspice
2 tablespoons water

Combine marinade ingredients in a bowl. Coat fish with marinade and refrigerate for 1-2 hours. Preheat broiler or prepare barbecue. Remove fish from marinade. Cook fish at medium heat, on both sides until golden brown, approximately 10 minutes. Heat marinade in small pan for 1 minute. Pour over grilled fish and serve. Serves 4.

Port Antonio Jerk Swordfish Kabobs
~ Jamaica ~

Marinade: 4 jalapeño or Scotch Bonnet Peppers, seeded and minced
2 tablespoons fresh thyme leaves
1 medium onion, diced
½ teaspoon ground nutmeg
½ cup red wine vinegar

6 green onions, diced
½ teaspoon ground allspice
¼ cup vegetable oil
1 teaspoon black peppercorns, crushed

¼ teaspoon ground cinnamon
¾ cup soy sauce
½ teaspoon ground cloves
¼ cup brown sugar

Kabobs: 1½ pounds swordfish steaks, cubed
1 green pepper, cut into chunks
1 large onion, cut into chunks

1 red bell pepper, cut into chunks

2 cups fresh pineapple, cubed

Make a marinade by combining all ingredients in a food processor fitted with a steel blade. Process for 15 seconds on high speed and set aside. Skewer alternately the onion, pineapple, peppers and swordfish cubes piercing the center of the ingredients. Repeat process until all of the ingredients are on skewers. Place kabobs in a shallow pan and pour marinade evenly over them. Refrigerate for 6 hours turning them after 3 hours. Preheat the grill until the coals are gray to white. Drain skewered kabobs and place on a lightly oiled grill. Cook for 7 minutes on each side, until fish is done in center. Serves 4.

Port au Prince Lambi Créole
~ Haiti ~

1 garlic clove, chopped
2 lemons, juiced
2 bird pepper chilies, chopped
2 tablespoons water
dash salt

1 pound conch meat, fresh, canned or frozen
2 medium tomatoes, peeled, seeded and chopped
dash freshly ground black pepper
1 small onion, chopped

1 sprig fresh thyme
2 tablespoons butter

Beat conch meat with a mallet for 15 minutes. Wash with water and lemon juice until the oily feel of the meat is gone. Cut conch into small pieces. Heat butter in a skillet and sauté chile, onion and garlic. Add in conch and remaining ingredients and cook until tender. Serve with rice. Serves 2.

Port of Spain Mango-Curried Shrimp
~ Trinidad ~

2 tablespoons butter, melted
1 mango, peeled, pitted and diced
2 garlic cloves, minced
1/8 teaspoon cayenne pepper

16 large shrimp, peeled, and deveined
1 large sweet potato, scrubbed and diced
1 tablespoon fresh ginger, minced
2 tablespoons curry powder

6 green onions, minced
1½ cups water
¼ teaspoon salt

Melt butter in a large saucepan. Add ginger, green onions and garlic. Sauté for 3 minutes. Add cayenne, salt and curry powder and sauté another 2 minutes. Pour in water and add sweet potato. Cook on medium heat for 15 minutes. Add in mango and shrimp and cook for 7 minutes, stirring frequently. Serves 2.

Red Snapper a la Créole
~ Martinique ~

2 red snappers or white-fleshed fish   2 limes, juiced

Spices: 1 onion, minced
1 garlic clove, crushed

1 red bell pepper, seeded and minced
dash freshly ground pepper

½ teaspoon ground allspice
dash salt

Dressing: 1 tablespoon capers
2 tablespoons vinegar

3 sprigs thyme, diced
6 tablespoons olive oil

2 sprigs parsley, diced
2 tomatoes, diced

Prepare a grill. Place fish in a bowl with enough water to cover and lime juice. Marinate for 5 minutes. Remove fish and allow to drain, pat dry. Season with spices. Cook on both sides until light brown. Combine the ingredients for the dressing in a bowl. Spoon cold dressing over cooked fish. Serves 4.

Saltfish and Ducana
~ Antigua ~

2 pounds saltfish
4 fluid ounces vegetable oil
¼ pound onion, chopped
½ hot pepper, seeded and chopped

3 garlic cloves
4 celery stalks, chopped
¼ pound green bell pepper, chopped
5 ounces tomatoes, sliced

4 ounces tomato paste
2 ounces butter
¼ bunch thyme, chopped

Boil the saltfish three times, each time using fresh water. Remove the fish and allow to cool down. With the back of your knife, skin the fish, remove bones and shred the fish. Set aside. Using an iron pot, heat oil and add butter, vegetables and thyme. Then add saltfish and simmer. Add tomato paste and stir well. Cook for 15 minutes. Remove from heat and serve with Ducana (see page: 52). Serves 4.

Saltfish Pie
~ Antigua ~

2 pounds saltfish, boiled and deboned
2 hard-boiled eggs, sliced
4 tablespoons mayonnaise
½ hot pepper, seeded and chopped

¾ pound yam, cooked
1¾ cups milk
4 tablespoons butter
dash freshly ground pepper

1 large onion, thinly sliced
3 large tomatoes, sliced
3 tablespoons ketchup
dash salt

Mash yam with milk and a dab of butter. Spread some of the mashed yam in the bottom of a greased pie dish. Add sliced yam, tomatoes, saltfish and onion in alternating layers. Top with salt, pepper, ketchup, mayonnaise and hot pepper and cover with egg slices. Dot with butter. On a floured board, roll out remaining mashed yam then cover pie carefully with yam. Decorate with fork and 1 tablespoon of butter. Bake at 400°F until brown. Serves 6.

Santo Domingo Red Snapper Fricassée
~ Dominican Republic ~

2 whole red snappers, (1½ to 2 pounds each), cleaned and scaled, with heads and tails attached
6 whole black peppercorns
1 tablespoon olive oil
1 onion, sliced thin
10 pimiento stuffed Spanish olives
1 tablespoon Worcestershire sauce

2 garlic cloves, crushed
1 teaspoon vinegar
2 bay leaves
1 (8 ounce) can tomato sauce

1 teaspoon dried oregano
½ cup vegetable oil
½ cup water
1 chicken bouillon cube

Rinse fish thoroughly with cold water and pat dry. Crush oregano, garlic and peppercorns together. Add olive oil and vinegar into mixture. Vertically slice each fish on both sides 3-4 times. Rub seasoning into skin. Heat vegetable oil in frying pan and brown fillets on both sides, approximately 3 minutes each. Add in onion, olives, bay leaves, bouillon cube, Worcestershire sauce and tomato sauce. Cook on high for another 5 minutes. Add water and boil. Cover and simmer for 10 minutes. Fish is done when it flakes easily with a fork. Serves 4-6.

Seafood a la Gros
~ Dominica ~

1 pound lobster meat
¾ cup water
1 tomato, chopped
1 tablespoon lime juice

2 tablespoons melted butter
4 scallions
1 tablespoon parsley, minced
1 hot pepper, seeded and chopped

2 garlic cloves, crushed
1 onion, chopped
1 teaspoon thyme, minced

Sauté lobster in melted butter until golden. Place lobster aside. Add crushed garlic to a pot of boiling water. Stir in the remainder of the ingredients except the lime juice and lobster. Simmer into a sauce for 15 minutes. Add in lobster and lime juice. Allow flavors to heat through. Serves 2.

Shipwreck Grouper with Fiery Eggplant Sauce
~ St. Martin ~

4 grouper fillets, 8 ounces each

1 lime, quartered

½ cup all-purpose flour

Sauce: 1 cup eggplant, diced
1 tomato, diced
½ cup okra, cooked and chopped
½ teaspoon red hot sauce
¼ cup canned tomatoes, crushed
⅛ teaspoon cayenne pepper

1 garlic clove, minced
¼ cup butter, melted, or vegetable oil
¼ cup water
½ cup onion, diced
⅛ teaspoon red pepper flakes
¼ teaspoon freshly ground black pepper

1 teaspoon oregano, dried
⅛ teaspoon salt
½ cup bell pepper, diced
¼ teaspoon white pepper

In a large saucepan, add 2 tablespoons of butter, garlic, onion, eggplant, tomato and bell pepper. Sauté on medium heat for 8 minutes, until vegetables are soft. Add in seasonings, okra, water and crushed tomatoes and bring to a simmer for 5 minutes on low heat, stirring frequently. Set aside. Heat a large skillet and add 2 tablespoons butter. Dredge fish fillets lightly in flour and place in skillet. Cook fillets on medium heat, 7 minutes on each side. Place fillets on serving plates and spoon eggplant sauce over the top. Garnish with lime wedges. Serves 4.

St. John Fry Fish
~ St. John ~

4 fish filets, 1 inch thick
Virgin Seasoning (see page: 22)
3 tomatoes, peeled, chopped
¼ cup water
dash hot pepper sauce

lime juice and water for rinsing
vegetable oil, for frying
¼ teaspoon fresh thyme
dash freshly ground pepper

3 onions, sliced
2 tablespoons tomato purée
½ cup vinegar
dash salt

Clean fish and rinse with lime juice and water. Split open on side, creating a deep pocket. Fill with Virgin Seasoning. Refrigerate for several hours or overnight. Pat the fish dry and sprinkle with salt. Fry in a pan with heated oil until both sides are golden brown. Remove from pan and pour off most of the oil. Sauté onions, tomatoes and thyme leaves in remaining oil. Add tomato purée, vinegar, spices to taste, hot pepper sauce to taste and water. Once blended, add fish and cover, simmer for 5 additional minutes. Serve hot. Serves 4.

St. John Plantain Grouper
~ U.S. Virgin Islands ~

4 grouper fillets, 8 ounces each
¼ cup vegetable oil
2 eggs, beaten
1 tablespoon Virgin Seasoning (see page: 22)

1 lime, quartered
¼ cup dry white wine
2 green plantains, peeled and sliced thinly

½ cup lime juice
¼ cup milk

Marinate grouper in wine and lime juice for 2 hours. Preheat oven to 200°F. Spread plantains out on baking sheet. Bake the plantains for 1½-2 hours until plantains are dry. Cool plantains and add to food processor fitted with a steel blade. Process for 30 seconds. Sift the resulting flour to avoid clumps. In a shallow dish, combine Island Seasoning with plantain flour. In another dish, add milk and eggs; mix well. Drown each fillet in the egg mixture and coat both sides with the plantain flour. In a large skillet, add 2 tablespoons of oil and heat to a sizzling point on medium heat. Place a couple fillets in the skillet and cook for 7 minutes on each side. Repeat process with remaining fish, adding a little more oil if necessary. Garnish with lime wedges and serve. Serves 4.

St. Thomas Curried Scallops
~ U.S. Virgin Islands ~

2 pounds sea scallops

Sauce: 2 garlic cloves
1 medium red bell pepper, chopped
1 Scotch Bonnet Pepper or jalapeño pepper, seeded and minced
2 teaspoons minced fresh ginger
½ teaspoon fresh ground pepper

1 cup cooked okra, chopped

2 tablespoons melted butter
2 tablespoons curry powder

½ teaspoon ground cloves
2 potatoes, scrubbed and chopped

2 tablespoons melted butter

1 teaspoon ground cumin
1 medium red onion, diced
2 cups water
¼ teaspoon salt
2 cups cooked chickpeas

For the sauce, place melted butter, red onion, bell pepper, garlic, Scotch Bonnet Pepper and ginger in a deep skillet and sauté for 5 minutes over medium heat. Add curry powder, cumin, cloves, black pepper and salt and sauté for an additional 2 minutes. Add potatoes and water and simmer for 15 minutes, or until potatoes are soft. Lower heat, add chickpeas and cook for another 10 minutes, or until the sauce is thick. Set aside. Place melted butter and scallops in a large skillet. Sauté over moderately high heat for 10 minutes. Add okra and cook for 2 more minutes. Add chickpea sauce. Simmer for 5 minutes, stirring frequently. Serve with rice. Makes 4 servings.

Yellowfin Tuna in Vanilla-Rum Flambé
~ Puerto Rico ~

2 (1 inch) yellowfin tuna steaks
dash ground cinnamon

1 freshly squeezed lime
1 tablespoon melted butter

adobo seasoning(see page: 18)
2 splashes vanilla rum

Vanilla rum: Soak 3 pods of vanilla in a quart of quality white rum for 3 weeks to create an infusion of flavors or add 1 teaspoon of pure vanilla extract to 1 cup of rum.

Tuna Steaks: Layer lime juice on top of tuna steaks with cinnamon and adobo. Melt butter in skillet. Place in seasoned tuna steaks and cook until golden brown on each side. Pour vanilla rum over the steaks and flambé. Serve with rice, fresh vegetables. Serves 2.

Meat

Bébélé
~ Martinique ~

1 breadfruit, peeled and cubed	14 ounces tripe, cut into 1 inch pieces	1 lemon, juiced
3 garlic cloves, crushed	1 whole hot pepper	3 green onions
2 sprigs fresh thyme, diced	2 sprigs fresh parsley, diced	water
4 ounces yams, peeled and cubed	4 pounds plantains, peeled and sliced	dash salt
1 tablespoon olive oil	1 French pork sausage (andouille), chopped into cubes	

Dumplings: 2¼ cups all-purpose flour   dash salt
½ teaspoon baking powder   1 cup water

Cover tripe with water in saucepan and squeeze in ¾ of the lemon juice. Boil for about 1-1½ hours, until tender. Drain cooking water. Add in about 6 cups fresh water, 2 garlic cloves, hot pepper and andouille sausage. Leave pepper whole. Add oil, green onions, thyme, parsley, plantains, breadfruit, yams, salt and remaining lemon juice into broth. Simmer partly covered for 25-30 minutes.

Dumplings: Sift flour, baking powder and salt into mixing bowl. Slowly add enough water to create a firm dough. Pull off small pieces from the dough and roll into small, round balls (approximately 1 teaspoonful). Gently place the dumplings into the simmering pot. Add the third clove of garlic and cook for a final 20-30 minutes. Mixture will be very thick when done. Serves 4.

Beef Pâté
~ Caribbean ~

Dough: 10 pounds plain flour	1 pound shortening, vegetable	5 ounces baking powder
3 cups cool water		

Meat Pâté Filling: 2 pounds lean ground beef		1 chopped onion
2 chopped stalks celery	½ chopped bell pepper	dash black pepper
dash garlic powder	dash oregano	dash parsley flakes
1 teaspoon salt	2 tablespoons tomato purée	½ chopped hot pepper

Dough: Mix all ingredients together thoroughly in a mixing bowl for 30 minutes. Set aside for 20 minutes.

Filling: In a large skillet, cook together all the ingredients for the beef pâté, allowing for flavors to blend well. The filling is ready when the vegetables are just soft and the meat is completely cooked. Drain off fat. Portion 4 ounce pieces of dough for each pâté. Roll with a rolling pin to flatten, place 1½ tablespoons of filling in each dough piece. Fold dough over pâté and seal by pressing down the ends with a fork. Trim with a dough cutter. Heat vegetable oil to 360°F and fry evenly until golden brown. Makes 4½ dozen.

Caribbean Best Steak
~ Dominica ~

4 strip steaks, 8 ounces each, well trimmed

Marinade: ½ cup rum
1 teaspoon ground allspice
2 teaspoons fresh ginger, minced
1 tablespoon fresh parsley, minced

1 teaspoon ground cloves
1 teaspoon red pepper flakes
¼ cup vegetable oil

¼ cup lime juice
¼ cup Worcestershire sauce
2 garlic cloves, minced

In a shallow baking dish, combine all of the ingredients for the marinade. Place steaks in marinade and refrigerate for 6 hours. Turn the steaks after 3 hours. Heat up grill until coals are gray to white. Place steaks on lightly oiled gill, cook for 5 minutes and turn. Continue grilling until you have reached desired degree of being done. Serve alone or with papaya mustard sauce or thyme mustard sauce. Serves 4.

Carnival Goat
~ Dominica ~

½ cup white vinegar
dash salt
1 tablespoon dried oregano
6 carrots, peeled and quartered
2 (12 ounce) cans light lager beer

3 pounds goat meat, trimmed and cut into bite size pieces
dash freshly ground pepper
½ cup olive oil
1 sprig parsley, chopped
4 tomatoes, peeled and quartered

3 garlic cloves, minced
1 (8 ounce) can tomato sauce
2 bay leaves
1 onion, chopped

Rinse goat meat with cold water and pat dry. Sprinkle meat with vinegar, cover and refrigerate overnight. Drain and rinse again in cold water and pat dry. Season with salt, pepper and oregano. Heat oil in a heavy saucepan. Add meat and brown on all sides. Add tomato sauce, onion, parsley, bay leaves and beer. Mix well. Bring to a boil, reduce heat and simmer for 1 hour. Add potatoes and carrots and simmer for an additional 30 minutes. Serves 4.

Glorious Baked Stuffed Papaya
~ Anguilla ~

1 green papaya, (about 4½ pounds)
1 onion, minced
1 hot pepper, seeded and minced
dash salt
lime wedges, to garnish

2 tablespoons olive oil
3 tomatoes peeled and chopped
1 teaspoon dried thyme
dash freshly ground pepper
1 tablespoon fresh bread crumbs

1 garlic clove, crushed
1 pound lean ground pork
¼ teaspoon ground allspice
4 tablespoons cheese, grated

Preheat oven to 350°F. Halve papaya lengthwise and scoop out seeds. Place papaya in a pan of boiling salt water and simmer for 10 minutes. Lift out and drain. Pat dry and arrange in a baking dish. Sauté onion and garlic in oil for 10 minutes. Stir in pork and brown evenly. Mix in hot pepper, tomatoes, allspice, thyme and seasoning. Cook 20 minutes or until thickened. Blend in half of the grated cheese. Spoon meat mixture into papaya halves. Toss together remaining cheese and breadcrumbs. Layer on tops of papaya halves. Bake until golden and a fork pierces papaya easily, about 30-40 minutes. Garnish with lime wedges and serve with tomato sauce on the side. Serves 6.

Grilled Crocodile
~ Cuba ~

2 fillets crocodile
2 onions, chopped
1 glass white wine

2 tablespoons butter
dash freshly ground pepper
dash salt

1 lime, juiced
Worcestershire sauce

In a sizzling hot, greased pan, sear the fillets on each side. Moisten occasionally with lime juice, butter, and onions. Season to taste and remove from pan, set aside. Make gravy by simmering together Worcester sauce and wine. Add a touch of butter. Slice the fillets into bite size pieces. Serve with fresh seasonal vegetables and homemade island bread. Serves 2.

Iguana Stew
~ Curaçao ~

Meat: 1 iguana, skinned and gutted, cut into bite size chunks
2 limes, juiced
whiskey

2 cups water

Seasonings: bay leaves
thyme, chopped
1 hot pepper, seeded and chopped

parsley, chopped
3-4 stalks celery, chopped
dash salt

chives, chopped
3 garlic cloves, crushed
1 cup fresh coconut milk

Vegetables: 10 potatoes, cubed
1 cup wide noodles

3 chopped tomatoes

3 chopped green peppers

Rub lime juice into iguana meat and soak for about 2 hours. Prepare a large pot of boiling water and portion in marinated iguana meat. Cook for about 30 minutes, clearing away cloudy excess from top of broth often. Add coconut milk and spices. Boil for an additional 20 minutes. Include remainder of ingredients, adding the whiskey as the final touch. Slowly cook in the flavors for 30 more minutes. Funchi cornbread (see page: 53) and Johnny Cakes (see page: 14) compliment this gourmet dish.

Island Sautéed Liver
~ Martinique ~

¼ cup flour
1 garlic clove, minced
2 tablespoons olive oil
¼ cup red wine
dash freshly ground black pepper

1 pound calf's liver, veins and membranes removed
1 large onion, thinly sliced
1 teaspoon Scotch Bonnet Chile, minced
1 branch thyme, crushed or ¼ teaspoon dried
2 tablespoons butter

Wash and cut liver into 1 inch pieces. In a large glass bowl, combine red wine, olive oil, black pepper, thyme, chile and garlic. Whisk all ingredients until well mixed. Add liver pieces in marinade and let them sit, covered, for 1 hour. In a large skillet, heat butter and add onion. Allow to cook until golden but not brown. Take pieces of liver out marinade, drain and coat with flour. Sauté them on each side until they have reached desired being done. Serve with white rice. Serves 4.

Jug Jug
~ Barbados ~

1 pound salted pork or pig's tail
16 cups pigeon peas
1 tied bunch of thyme, marjoram and chives

1 pound salted beef
2½ cups guinea corn

1 tablespoon butter
½ pound onions, chopped

Soak salted meat in water overnight. Boil meat in a pot of fresh water. Change water. Repeat process until salt has been removed. Add tied seasonings, peas and onion. Boil until meat and peas are tender. Remove peas and place in a separate bowl. Remove the meat from the pot, debone and mince. Mince peas and add to meat. In a little cold water, mix guinea corn until free of lumps. Pour part of the water from peas and salted meat into a pot. Cook over medium heat, add guinea corn, stirring slowly. Stir until cooked and has the consistency of porridge. Add in minced peas, butter and meat. Serve warm. Serves 4-6.

Karni Kabritu Stobá
~ Aruba ~

2 pounds goat or lamb, cubed
1 onion, minced
2 teaspoons tomato purée (paste)
¾ cup water
1 tablespoon white vinegar

1 tablespoon lime juice
2 garlic cloves, minced
1 hot pepper, seeded and minced
dash freshly ground pepper

3 tablespoons melted butter
1 tomato, chopped
¼ teaspoon paprika
dash salt

Sprinkle meat with lime juice and place in a bowl. Melt butter in a pan and brown meat evenly on all sides over medium heat. Add garlic and onion to meat and fry for one minute. Add the rest of the ingredients and cook 5 more minutes. Preheat oven to 350°F and place the prepared meat dish into a large casserole. Cover and cook for 45 minutes until meat is soft and juicy. Funchi (see page: 53) and fried plantains make this a taste sensation. Serves 4.

Keshi Yena
~ Curaçao ~

2 pounds ground beef
2½ pounds edam cheese
2 onions, sliced
¼ cup stuffed olives, sliced
1 tablespoon parsley
2 teaspoons Worcestershire sauce
1 tablespoon tomato paste

3 tomatoes, peeled and chopped
1 garlic clove
1 green bell pepper, chopped
2 tablespoons ketchup
¼ hot red pepper, minced or dash Tabasco sauce
dash freshly ground pepper

5 eggs
¼ cup raisins or prunes
2 tablespoons piccalilly
1 tablespoon capers

dash salt

Fry the ground meat. Fry vegetables in another pan, then add to meat. Add all seasonings. In a small bowl beat the eggs and add to meat and vegetables, reserving a small amount to seal cheese. Add raisins or prunes. Cut a hole ("lid") in rind of cheese and scoop out inside. The hollowed rind should be about ½ inch thick. Put meat mixture in cheese rind. Spread remaining egg on top of cheese as a sealer and cover with the lid. Place cheese in a casserole dish. Place casserole dish in a pan of hot water. Bake at 350ºF for 1½ hours. Serves 4.

Key West Garden-Style Veal Chops
~ Florida Keys ~

4 veal chops
1 teaspoon dried oregano
3 tablespoons olive oil
1 green bell pepper, seeded, chopped
2 medium tomatoes, thinly sliced

1 garlic clove, peeled
½ teaspoon salt
1 carrot
1 red bell pepper, seeded, chopped
1 (8 ounce) can tomato sauce

6 whole black peppercorns
½ teaspoon white vinegar
1 onion, chopped

Rinse chops in cold water and pat dry. Pound in a mortar: peppercorns, garlic, oregano and salt, until crushed. Blend in 2 tablespoons olive oil and vinegar. Rub chops with seasonings. Marinate for 10 minutes. In a frying pan, heat 1 tablespoon of olive oil and add chops. Brown evenly on both sides. Add remaining vegetables and tomato sauce. Bring to a boil. Cover and simmer for 20 minutes.

Komkomber Stoba
~ Curaçao ~

3 pounds lamb or beef
2 onions, chopped
2 green bell peppers, chopped
8 tablespoons butter
1 (14 ounce) can tomatoes
Worcestershire sauce

6-8 cups komkomber, (similar to cucumber)
1 pound salted beef
1 tablespoon sugar
dash nutmeg, onion powder, garlic, freshly ground pepper and salt
1 tablespoon tomato paste
Maggi

2 garlic cloves, minced
1 pound potatoes, cubed

1 tablespoon vegetable oil

Wash and remove stems from komkombers. Cut each komkomber into 4-6 wedges and remove seeds. In a pot, boil salted beef twice, changing water after the first boil. Prepare beef and lamb with all seasonings. Heat a large pot with a little oil. Brown meats and seasonings, add remaining ingredients and a little water. Simmer until stew is ready. Serves 6.

Lechon Asado
~ Puerto Rico ~

12-14 pound suckling pig, cleaned or large pork pieces
2 tablespoons fresh oregano, finely chopped
2 tablespoons marjoram, finely chopped
2 tablespoons sour orange juice

10 garlic cloves, minced
3 tablespoons salt
2 tablespoons water

Wash meat well and cut deep gashes in it. Combine remaining ingredients to form a paste. Press seasoning paste into gashes. If whole pig is used, put paste in cavity also. Refrigerate overnight. Place pig in a roasting pan, cover with foil and then place on the roasting rack of a preheated 325°F oven. Baste occasionally. Roast for 4-5 hours. When a skewer is inserted in the meat and juices run clear, remove foil and cook for an additional 20-30 minutes or until the meat is browned. Rest meat at room temperature for 10-15 minutes before carving. Serves 10-12.

_____

Leg of Lamb with Mint-Guava Sauce
~ Virgin Islands ~

6-8 pounds leg of lamb
1 tablespoon mint jelly
6 slices of stewed guava

4 tablespoons guava jelly
2 tablespoons Virgin Seasoning (see page: 22)
dash salt and freshly ground pepper

1 tablespoon rum

Mix salt, pepper, jellies, rum and seasoning together. Cut deep slices into the lamb and stuff with seasoning. Refrigerate overnight. Preheat oven to 400°F. Place the lamb in a greased roasting pan and bake for 10 minutes. Reduce heat to 350°F. Bake for 20 minutes per pound. When done, garnish with slices of stewed guava.

Gravy: Pour juices of roasting pan into a saucepan. Warm over medium heat and add a tablespoon of flour. Stir into a paste. Add 1 cup of water until gravy thickens. Add salt and pepper. Serves 12.

_____

Mango Mojo Pork
~ Key West, Florida Keys ~

2 tablespoons virgin olive oil
1 tablespoon salt
2 cups Mango Mojo (see page: 20)

2 pounds pork tenderloin, trim off excess fat
½ tablespoons fresh ground pepper
4 yellow plantains, peeled, cut into 2 inch pieces

Place pork in baking dish. Pour mango mojo over meat, cover and refrigerate 2-24 hours. Preheat oven to 400°F. Drain and set marinade aside. Gently dry pork with paper towels. Brush the pork with olive oil and season with salt and pepper. Roast pork in a roasting pan for 10 minutes. Decrease temperature to 350°F and turn pork over. Pour half of the marinade over meat. Add plantains and roast for 35-45 minutes, or until pork is cooked. Serves 4.

Negril Curry Goat
~ Jamaica ~

2½ cups water
1 garlic clove, minced
1 shallot, minced
2 onions, chopped
1 scallion, green top, minced
2 tablespoons butter

2 pounds goat or mutton, cut into 1 inch cubes
¼ cup vegetable oil for frying
2 large tomatoes, peeled, seeded and chopped
dash salt and freshly ground black pepper
3 tablespoons Madras-type curry powder
1 Scotch Bonnet Chile, seeded and minced

In a large bowl, place meat with curry powder, salt, pepper, onions, garlic, tomatoes, shallot, scallion and chile. Mix together well and allow meat to marinate for 30 minutes. In a large skillet heat butter and oil. Remove meat from marinade. Reserve marinade. Brown the meat. Add the marinade and water, then cover. Cook over medium heat for 1½ hours until meat is tender. Serve with white rice. Serves 4.

Passaat Roast Lamb
~ Curaçao ~

2 young lambs
1 cup oil
2 garlic cloves

12 hot peppers
1 cup white wine vinegar
4 cloves

2 large onions
1 cup tomato juice
1 teaspoon salt

Split the underside of lambs, leaving backs intact. Discard organs and wash and dry meat. Espalier lambs on two double T-frames. Build a large fire on the ground with charcoal. When flames die down, pound the frames into the ground three feet windward of coals. The constant breeze permeates the meat with charcoal flavor. Baste lambs frequently with barbeque sauce. Roast for four hours, keeping charcoals very hot. Barbeque Sauce: Combine hot peppers, onions and oil. Place in a jar. Bring to a boil rest of ingredients and pour the hot mixture in jar. Cover and set aside. Make sauce four days in advance. Serves 30.

Picadillo
~ Cuba ~

2 pounds ground beef, lean
2 garlic cloves, minced
¼ teaspoon cumin
8 olives, pimento stuffed
2 ounces seedless raisins
1 tablespoon cilantro, finely chopped

¼ cup vegetable oil
2 seeded hot peppers, finely chopped
1 medium green bell pepper, seeded and finely chopped
1 tablespoon lemon juice or dry white wine
1 tablespoon tomato purée (or tomato paste)
1 tablespoon fresh parsley, chopped

1 large onion, chopped finely
¼ cup beef stock

½ teaspoon dried oregano

Place meat in a pot. Add 1 teaspoon of salt and enough water to cover meat. Boil about 20 minutes or until meat is tender. In a large frying pan, heat oil over medium heat. Add onion, garlic, hot peppers, green bell pepper, cilantro and cumin. Sauté approximately 4 minutes or until onion is tender. Stir in meat, 1 teaspoon salt and remaining ingredients. Cook on low heat for 10 minutes. Serves 4

Point Fortin Lamb Pie
~ Trinidad ~

1 pound puff pastry dough
¼ cup fresh mint leaves, minced
¼ teaspoon ground turmeric
1 teaspoon fresh thyme leaves
3 garlic cloves, minced
1 lime, juiced

1 pound lamb, cubed and well trimmed
1 medium onion, diced
2 tablespoons curry powder
½ teaspoon ground coriander
1 cup potatoes, diced, unpeeled and scrubbed
1 chile pepper, seeded and minced

2 tablespoons butter
½ cup water
½ teaspoon ground allspice
2 tomatoes, diced

Preheat oven to 400°F. In a skillet, add butter, garlic and onion and sauté for 2 minutes. Add in seasonings, tomatoes and chile pepper. Sauté 2 more minutes. Stir in lime juice, lamb and potatoes and cook for 10 minutes. Stir frequently. Pour in water and cook 5 minutes. Add in the mint leaves and stir occasionally. Roll out pastry dough into two 10 inch round circles. Arrange one layer in the bottom of a 9 inch round cake pan covering sides of pan as well as the bottom. Spread lamb mixture over dough. Cover the filling with the remaining circle of dough. To seal, pinch the edges together. Bake for 15 minutes until crust is lightly brown. Serves 6-8.

Rabbit Fricassée
~ Puerto Rico ~

1 lemon, halved
½ pound lean cured ham
3 tablespoons sofrito, (see page: 22)
10 pimento stuffed Spanish olives
2 pounds potatoes, peeled and cubed
6 ounce jar pimentos, drained and cut into strips

dash freshly ground pepper
2 garlic cloves, minced
2 bay leaves
8 ounce can tomato sauce
1 rabbit (3 pounds) cut into serving size pieces

½ cup olive oil
1 cup dry red wine
¾ cup warm water
dash salt

Wash rabbit pieces and pat dry. In a bowl, place rabbit and sprinkle with lemon. Marinate for 10 minutes and drain. In a saucepan, add rabbit, salt, pepper, garlic and olive oil. Sauté for 5 minutes over medium heat. Add sofrito, ham, olives, tomato sauce, bay leaves and ½ cup warm water. Bring to a boil, cover and simmer for 30 minutes. Stir occasionally. Add wine, pimentos, potatoes and ¼ cup warm water. Bring to a boil, cover and simmer for and additional 20 minutes. Remove bay leaves before serving. Serves 6.

Ragoût De Boeuf
~ Martinique ~

3 tablespoons olive oil
1 scallion, diced
1 whole hot pepper
¼ teaspoon ground allspice
1 tablespoon tomato purée

2 pounds beef, cubed
2 garlic cloves, crushed
2 tablespoons parsley, chopped
1 bay leaf
dash salt and white pepper

1 onion, diced
¼ cup water
3 sprigs thyme
1 tablespoon white vinegar
1 teaspoon lime juice

In deep frying pan, heat oil over medium high heat. Sauté beef until evenly browned on each side. Add onions and garlic to beef and sauté. Add spices, tomato purée, bay leaf, herbs and liquid ingredients. Stir. Simmer for 45-60 minutes, until meat is soft. Discard bay leaf, hot pepper and thyme stems. Serve hot. Serves 4.

Roasted Wild Pig with Red Wine Sauce
~ Dominica ~

3½ pounds wild pig (leg or loin)
3 garlic cloves, minced
dash salt
1 tablespoon butter

½ bottle red wine
1 tablespoon fresh ginger, minced
dash freshly ground pepper
¼ teaspoon hot pepper, seeded and crushed

1 onion, minced
2 sprigs chives, chopped
½ cup wild pig stock

Marinate meat in wine overnight. Remove meat from marinade and reserve wine. Preheat oven to 350°F. Crush the seasonings with a mortar and pestle. Score and stuff meat evenly with half of the seasoning mixture. Place in a slightly greased roasting pan and cook for half an hour. Add the stock, basting thoroughly. Cover with aluminum foil and cook for another hour and 15 minutes. Baste at least twice during this period. Add half the wine and a tablespoon of butter about half an hour before meat is done. Remove from oven, baste and let rest in its juices for 15 minutes before slicing. Serves 6.

Ropa Vieja
~ Cuba ~

2 pounds leftover meat, shredded
¼ cup olive oil
1 large tomato, chopped
1 tablespoon tomato purée

1 teaspoon salt
1 large onion, minced
½ green bell pepper, seeded and chopped
1 teaspoon fresh oregano, chopped

2 garlic cloves, crushed
1 tablespoon capers

Use salt and garlic to season the meat. Place oil in saucepan and heat to a medium high heat. Sauté onion and green pepper until onion is translucent, about 1 minute. Slowly mix in tomato, tomato purée and fresh oregano. Cook flavors together for 5 minutes. Add meat, hot pepper and capers. Reduce heat and simmer for 8 minutes, stirring occasionally. Serves 4.

San Juan's Piononos con Plantanos
~ Puerto Rico ~

3 ripened plantains, peeled

2 beaten eggs

vegetable oil, for frying

Filling: 1 pound lean ground beef
1 onion, minced
1 small green bell pepper, minced
dash salt
8 pimiento stuffed olives, chopped

2 ounces ground ham
2 tomatoes, peeled and chopped
1 tablespoon fresh oregano
dash freshly ground pepper
1 tablespoon capers, chopped

1 garlic clove, crushed
1 tablespoon olive oil
½ lime, juiced

Quarter each plantain lengthwise into slices. Fry in hot oil for 4 minutes until each side is golden. Drain and allow to cool enough to handle. With each slice, form a circle and secure with a toothpick. Set to the side. Sauté onion and garlic in oil for 10 minutes. Mix beef in with onion and garlic until brown. Add in ham, seasoning, oregano, green bell pepper, lime juice and tomatoes. Stir often and cook until thickened, about 10-15 minutes. When finished, mix in olives and capers. Spoon filling into plantain rings and coat sides of plantains with beaten egg. Place a few platain rings in a skillet and fill with oil half way up plantains. Cook until golden brown on each side about 3-4 minutes each. Repeat process until all plantains are cooked. Great with rice and peas. Serves 6.

Saté
~ Aruba ~

2 garlic cloves
1 teaspoon ground coriander for beef or 1 teaspoon ground ginger for pork
1 large onion, coarsely chopped
2 tablespoons sugar
36 skewers

5 pounds beef or pork tenderloin, cubed

1 teaspoon salt
1¼ cups soy sauce

2 tablespoons soy sauce
2 lemons, juiced
2 cups vegetable oil

In a blender or food processor, combine garlic, onion, lemon juice, sugar, salt, 1 cup oil, 1 cup soy sauce and coriander or ginger. Blend well and pour over meat. Marinate for 2 hours. Remove meat from marinade and place on skewers. Place skewers in a shallow dish. Blend 1 cup oil and ¼ cup soy sauce. Pour over meat to keep juicy before cooking. Cook meat until done on the barbecue. Serves 8.

Savory Palomilla Steak
~ Florida Keys ~

1 pound top sirloin
¼ teaspoon freshly ground pepper
¼ cup finely chopped fresh parsley

2 tablespoons sour orange juice
¼ teaspoon salt

3 garlic cloves, peeled
¼ cup finely chopped onion

Using a mortar, combine garlic, salt and pepper into a paste with sour orange juice. Pound steak and cut into four pieces. Marinate meat with paste for one hour in refrigerator. Rinse steaks and reserve marinade. Fry steaks in a skillet until golden brown. Drizzle with heated marinade. Serves 4.

St. George Garlic Pork
~ Guyana ~

4 pounds pork loin, cut in 1 inch pieces
6 cloves
2 cups cold water
1 tablespoon vegetable oil

½ pound garlic cloves, peeled
4 stalks thyme, or 1 teaspoon dried

3 cups white vinegar
2 teaspoons salt
2 Scotch Bonnet Chilies

Wash the pork pieces with vinegar in a large bowl. Place pork in a large jar or bottle using utensils. In a mortar, add thyme, peeled garlic and chilies. Pound to a paste. Add remaining vinegar and cold water to garlic mixture. Add cloves and salt and pour over pork, covering completely. Close jar and allow to marinate in a cool place 4 days or longer. Cook pork in a heavy skillet until liquid evaporates. Add vegetable oil and fry until brown. Serve over white rice. Serves 6-8.

Sweet Pork Tenderloin
~ Florida Keys ~

2 pork tenderloins
½ cup Worcestershire sauce

½ cup soy sauce
1 cup ketchup

1 cup honey

Preheat oven to 350ºF. Place tenderloins on a baking pan and bake for 30 minutes. Combine liquid ingredients and baste, reserving some sauce for serving. Bake for an additional 30 minutes. Before serving, pour remaining sauce over meat. Serves 6.

Trinidad Style Curried Lamb
~ Trinidad ~

1¾ pounds lamb shoulder, trimmed and cut 1 inch cubes
3 garlic cloves, crushed
2 teaspoons curry powder
2 teaspoons molasses
1 tablespoon fresh cilantro, chopped

1 onion, chopped
1 tablespoon hot pepper sauce
2 tablespoons tomato purée
dash salt

1 lime, juiced and rind grated
3 tablespoons olive oil
1 teaspoon ground cumin
2 ounces creamed coconut

Marinate lamb in lime juice, rind and garlic. Cover and refrigerate for at least 2 hours. In a skillet, sauté onion in oil on low heat for 10 minutes. Remove and set aside. Drain lamb and pat dry. Save the marinade. Fry meat and onion in hot oil until browned. Stir in curry and cumin, cooking on low for about a minute. Blend in molasses, tomato purée, hot sauce and creamed coconut. Cook for another 5 minutes. Pour in ⅔ cup of salted water, covering the meat. Bring to a boil and simmer, covered, for 1½-2 hours or until tender. Mix in cilantro. Great with Johnny Cakes (see page: 14) or white rice. Serves 4.

Veal Chops a la Jardinera
~ Cuba ~

4 veal chops, ¾ pound each
1 teaspoon dried oregano
½ teaspoon white vinegar
1 (16 ounce) can mixed vegetables, drained or fresh vegetables

6 whole peppercorns
dash salt
2 medium tomatoes, thinly sliced

1 garlic clove, peeled
3 tablespoons olive oil
1 (8 ounce) can tomato sauce

Rinse chops and pat dry. Combine peppercorns, garlic, oregano, salt and thyme in a mortar and crush. Rub chops with seasoning. In a skillet, heat oil and brown chops on each side; about 5 minutes per side. Remove and set aside. Add onion, bell pepper, tomatoes and bay leaves to drippings in skillet. Sauté for 5 minutes. Add chops, cover and simmer for 30 minutes. Serves 4.

Virgin Kallaloo
~ Virgin Islands ~

½ pound salted beef
½ pound ham bone
12 okra

½ pound pig's tail
2 whole clean crabs
3 pounds spinach or mixed greens

1 salted conch
1½ pounds fresh fish, cleaned
1 seeded hot pepper

Put beef and pig's tail in a large bowl with cold water and let soak overnight. Drain the water. Add 3 quarts of fresh water to a pot and boil beef, pork and conch together until tender. Add the clean fish and cook for 5 minutes. Remove the fish with a slotted spoon. Remove the bones, slice the fish into pieces, then put back into pot. Wash crab with water and lime and add to pot. Wash spinach and grind with okra. Add to pot with the hot pepper. Boil on high heat for 30 minutes. Add a dash of vinegar to remove the surface film. Serves 4.

Poultry

Arroz con Pollo
~ Cuba ~

3 pounds chicken pieces
dash freshly ground black pepper
3 tablespoons olive oil
¼ teaspoon paprika
1 cup dry white wine

2 garlic cloves, crushed
¼ teaspoon dried oregano
1 medium onion, chopped finely
½ green bell pepper, chopped
¼ cup tomato purée

1 lemon, juiced
¼ teaspoon cumin
1 bay leaf
2 cups rice, uncooked
4 cups chicken stock

Season chicken with garlic, lemon juice, pepper, cumin and oregano. In a large saucepan, heat oil over medium heat. Sauté bell pepper and onion until onion is translucent. Add seasoned chicken pieces and brown evenly on all sides. Pour off any excess fat. Stir in remaining ingredients except rice. Bring to a boil and then reduce to a simmering heat for 10 minutes. Add rice. Boil for 3 minutes, reduce heat and cover. Cook for 25 minutes. Serve hot. Serves 6.

Asopao de Pollo
~ Dominican Republic ~

3 pounds chicken pieces
dash paprika
2 teaspoons olive oil
8 pimiento stuffed olives
8 cups chicken stock

1 cup rice, uncooked
2 teaspoons salt
1 teaspoon white vinegar
1 tomato, chopped
2 tablespoons tomato purée (or paste)

1 teaspoon oregano, diced
2 garlic cloves, crushed
1 cup sofrito (see page: 22)
1 tablespoon capers

Garnish: ½ cup green peas, cooked   1 red bell pepper, sliced and cooked   ½ cup asparagus tips, cooked

Soak rice in cold water with 1 inch extra coverage. In a small bowl, mix together oregano, paprika, salt, garlic, oil and vinegar. Coat chicken pieces and rub in for flavor. Set aside and let soak for 30 minutes. Blend olives, tomato purée, capers and sofrito seasoning in a large saucepan over moderate heat. Add in chicken pieces and simmer, covered, for 20 minutes. Cooking chicken evenly on all sides. Add stock and bring to a boil on high heat. Drain soaked rice and stir into mixture. Turn down temperature to low, cover and cook for 15-20 minutes until rice is tender, stirring occasionally. Garnish with peas, asparagus and slices of red pepper. Serves 6.

Bayan-Rum Chicken
~ Barbados ~

1 cup dark rum
2 teaspoons red hot sauce
1 teaspoon paprika
¼ cup vegetable oil
2 teaspoons island seasoning
2 tablespoons thyme leaves

2 pounds chicken breast, skinless, boneless and cut into strips
3 Scotch Bonnet Peppers or jalapeño peppers, seeded and minced
½ cup lime juice
2 medium red onions, diced
2 tablespoons parsley, minced

¼ teaspoon salt
½ teaspoon black pepper
5 cloves garlic, minced

In a food processor, add black pepper, salt, lime juice, rum, red and green onions, garlic, red hot sauce, island seasonings, oil, thyme and parsley. Process for 20 seconds. Pour mixture into a bowl, add chicken and refrigerate for 6 hours. Preheat your grill until coals are gray to white. Oil the grill lightly. Take chicken out of marinade and drain. Place on the grill and cook for 5 minutes on each side or until done in the center. Serve with sweet plantain, black bean soup or saffron-scented soup. Serves 4.

Cassava Pie
~ Bermuda ~

Crust: 5 pounds cassava flour   12 eggs   1 pound butter
2 cups sugar   1 teaspoon salt   dash nutmeg

Filling: 2 pounds chicken   ¼ teaspoon fresh parsley, chopped 1 garlic clove, diced
¼ teaspoon fresh thyme, chopped   1 small onion, diced   ¼ teaspoon hot pepper, diced
1 sprig chives, diced finely   dash freshly ground pepper   dash salt

Blend all crust ingredients to form a sponge-like pastry. Grease and flour a 10 inch pie plate and line with half of the mixture. In a pot, boil chicken in 3 cups of water with remaining ingredients. When meat is cooked, drain liquid. Debone and cut meat into small pieces. Add to pie plate and spread evenly. Top with remaining cassava mixture to make another layer. Bake at 350°F for 2½ hours. Serves 6.

Cha-Cha-Cha-Chicken
~ Florida Keys ~

¾ cup olive oil   3 chicken breasts, split, boned and skinned
1 egg, beaten   1 tablespoon vinegar   1 garlic clove, crushed
¼ cup butter   1 cup bread crumbs   ½ cup coconut flakes

Wash chicken and pat dry. Pound chicken to about ¼ inch thickness between two sheets of wax paper. Combine in a bowl: egg, ½ cup olive oil, vinegar and garlic. Place breadcrumbs and coconut flakes on a plate. Dip chicken in egg-oil mixture and then in coconut breadcrumbs, coat evenly. In a frying pan, heat butter and ¼ cup olive oil. Cook breaded chicken until flaky and golden brown. Serves 4.

Chicken Mango Supreme
~ Bahamas ~

1 bottle chablis wine   3 boneless, skinless chicken breasts, quartered
4 ounces butter   2 medium mangoes, peeled and sliced lengthwise into spears
4 large garlic cloves, crushed   ¼ teaspoon cinnamon   2 tablespoons soy sauce

Pour wine into a large pan. Poach chicken breasts on high heat for 7 minutes. Pour off liquid, reserve 1 cup. Add butter and garlic and slowly pan-fry chicken until golden brown. Return reserve liquid and add soy sauce, orange juice, mangoes and cinnamon. Cover and simmer for 10 minutes. Makes 4 servings.

Colombo de Poulet
~ Guadeloupe ~

2 pounds chicken pieces
2 green onions, chopped finely
2 tablespoons curry powder
1 teaspoon dried thyme
¼ cup dried chickpeas (soaked overnight and drained before preparing recipe)
1 hot pepper, seeded and minced

1 medium onion, chopped finely
2 garlic cloves, minced
1 tablespoon white wine vinegar
1 tablespoon fresh parsley, minced

¼ cup peanut oil
½ teaspoon ground allspice
2 cups water
1 carrot, diced
2 zucchini, sliced

In a large saucepan, brown chicken in oil. Reduce to medium high heat and add garlic and onions. Cook until soft. Add chickpeas, thyme, vinegar, allspice, curry powder, parsley and water. Cover and cook on low heat for 40 minutes. Add diced carrot, sliced zucchini and hot pepper. Cook until all vegetables are tender. Serve while hot. Serves 4-6.

Créole Chicken Liver
~ Dominican Republic ~

1 pound chicken livers
1 teaspoon paprika
¼ cup light cream
dash freshly ground pepper

3 tablespoons olive oil
1 tablespoon flour
2 tablespoons dry sherry

1 onion, chopped
½ cup beef broth
dash salt

Rinse and pat dry livers. Remove any connective tissue. Sauté onion in a skillet until translucent. Add livers and cook for about 8 minutes over high heat, stirring occasionally. Add paprika, flour, broth, cream and sherry. Stir quickly. Season with salt and pepper. Serves 4.

Curried Chicken
~ Trinidad ~

¼ cup butter, melted
2 cups chickpeas, cooked
2 teaspoons ginger, minced
1½ cups water
1 teaspoon ground thyme

1½ pounds chicken breast, skinless, boneless, pounded and diced
2 garlic cloves, minced
½ teaspoon red hot sauce
2 tablespoons curry powder
2 sweet potatoes, scrubbed and diced

dash salt
1 small onion, diced
2 teaspoons ground cumin

In a deep skillet, sauté 2 tablespoons of butter, onion, garlic and ginger for 3 minutes over medium heat. Add in thyme, curry powder and cumin and sauté another minute. Pour in water and add hot sauce, potatoes and salt. Cook for 15 minutes until potatoes are soft but not mushy. Add the chickpeas and cook 10 minutes. In another skillet, add remaining butter and chicken and sauté on medium heat for 7 minutes until chicken is white in the center. Add to the vegetable curry mixture and bring to a simmer. Serve with white rice. Serves 4.

Drunken Quail
~ Key West, Florida Keys ~

8 quails	4 tablespoons dark rum	1 teaspoon molasses
4 tablespoons raisins	1 garlic clove, sliced	1 tablespoon virgin olive oil
1 onion, sliced	1 cup chicken stock	2 teaspoons arrowroot
dash freshly ground pepper	chopped fresh cilantro, to garnish	dash salt

In a container, soak raisins in rum for 2 hours. In a large frying pan, heat oil and add quail. Cook and turn until evenly browned. Remove quail and set aside. In same pan, add onion and garlic, cooking for 10 minutes. Strain rum from raisins, reserving raisins for garnish. Add rum to a separate saucepan, heat gently then light on fire to burn off alcohol. When flames die down, stir in molasses, stock and seasoning. Return quail to frying pan, add rum molasses stock. Cover and cook 20-30 minutes on medium heat, until thoroughly cooked. Place quail on serving dish and keep warm. In a bowl, mix arrowroot with a little water and stir into sauce in frying pan cook, stirring for a few minutes until sauce thickens. Pour over quail. Garnish with chopped cilantro and raisins. Serves 4.

———————————————

Essequibo Chicken
~ Guyana ~

2 pounds chicken pieces	1 teaspoon raw sugar	3 tablespoons vegetable oil
3 garlic cloves, crushed	1 onion, chopped	¼ teaspoon celery salt
¼ teaspoon garlic salt	2 sprigs thyme, chopped finely	2 green onions, chopped
1 medium tomato, chopped	1 tablespoon tomato purée	1¼ cups water
2 teaspoons cornstarch	¼ teaspoon freshly ground black pepper	
1 bay leaf, bruised	¼ red bell pepper, seeded and cut into thin strips	

In a large saucepan, heat oil over medium heat. When hot, sprinkle sugar over oil and let bubble for about 30 seconds. Add chicken pieces. Fry and brown evenly. Add onion and garlic. Fry for 1 minute. Stir in celery salt, garlic salt, green onions, thyme and bell pepper. Add bay leaf and tomato. Cook for 2 minutes. Add tomato purée and all but 2 tablespoons of water. Simmer on low heat and cook for 20 minutes. Combine cornstarch with remaining water and quickly stir into chicken mixture. Mix well and season with pepper. Cook until sauce is thickened. Serves 4.

———————————————

Fricasséed Chicken
~ St.Kitts ~

1 (5 pound) chicken, cut into pieces	2 tablespoons hot water
1 garlic clove, minced	3 medium size onions, 2 chopped, 1 sliced
1-inch fresh ginger, minced	3 scallions, including green tops, chopped
½ cup vegetable oil for frying	1 Scotch Bonnet Chile, pricked with a fork
dash freshly ground black pepper	3 medium size tomatoes, peeled, seeded and chopped
½ teaspoon paprika	dash salt

Wash chicken and pat dry. Mix ginger, salt, pepper, scallions and sliced onion to make marinade. Rub marinade on chicken pieces and refrigerate overnight. Before cooking, remove seasoning from chicken and wipe dry. Heat oil in a large skillet and brown chicken on all sides. Pour out most of remaining cooking oil. Add chopped onions, remaining ingredients and a dash of salt. On low heat, cover and simmer chicken for 45 minutes. Add a little water so mixture remains moist. Serves 6.

Jerk Chicken
~ Jamaica ~

3 pounds chicken pieces
3 scallions, chopped
2 hot peppers, seeded and chopped
2 tablespoons soy sauce
2 tablespoons water

1½ teaspoons ground allspice
1 onion, chopped
¼ teaspoon fresh ginger, grated
1½ teaspoons salt
6 tablespoons vegetable oil

¼ teaspoon ground cinnamon
3 garlic cloves, crushed
2 sprigs fresh thyme
½ teaspoon pepper

Blend spices together. Finely chop and mix garlic, onions, hot pepper, ginger and thyme into a bowl. Add spices, soy sauce, water, salt and pepper, and crush into a paste consistency. Coat chicken with seasoned paste in a large baking dish. Refrigerate covered for 3 hours. Prepare oven at 350°F. Sprinkle coated chicken with oil and bake for about 50 minutes, uncovered. Serves 6.

Las Olas Chicken
~ Key Largo, Florida Keys ~

2 pounds skinless chicken breasts

Marinade: 12 ounces Naranja Agria tamari soy sauce
dash red hot sauce

extra virgin olive oil

Salsa: 1 minced onion
dash cilantro
2 tablespoons garlic, crushed
½ lime, juiced

1 cup mango, chopped
extra virgin olive oil
1 jalapeño pepper

1 cup pineapple, chopped
1 teaspoon ginger, grated
fresh cut mint leaves, to taste

Mix together all marinade ingredients. Stir in chicken, refrigerate and allow to soak for 1 hour. Toss all salsa ingredients together, except lime juice, blending well. Prepare marinated chicken on the grill. Arrange on serving platter and spoon salsa on top. Sprinkle fresh lime juice as the final garnish flavor. Serves 6.

Paradise Fowl
~ Florida Keys ~

6 boneless, skinless chicken breasts
¼ cup white wine

1 cup sour cream

½ cup Dijon mustard

In a baking dish, spread out chicken breasts. Combine all other ingredients and spoon mixture over chicken. Cover with foil. Bake for 40 minutes at 350°F. For the last 10 minutes, remove foil. Serves 4.

Pelau Rice
~ Jamaica ~

1 pound chicken parts
2 green onions, chopped
2 tablespoons margarine
dash ground pepper
1 sprig thyme, finely chopped
½ red pepper, seeded and chopped

8 ounces salted beef or cubed corn beef
1 large onion, chopped
1 tablespoon soy sauce
1 cup dried pigeon peas or red peas
6 ounces pumpkin, cleaned, seeded and chopped
3 cups rinsed rice (rinse until water almost runs clear)

¼ cup vegetable oil
2 garlic cloves, crushed
1 tablespoon ketchup
dash salt

Soak peas overnight and drain just before preparing recipe. Soak beef for 1 hour in enough water to cover. Drain. In a large saucepan, heat oil over medium high heat. Add chicken to oil and fry for 2 minutes. Add beef, onions, thyme, garlic, pumpkin and bell pepper. Stir in rice, margarine, soy sauce and ketchup. Add salt and pepper to taste and fry for 3 minutes. Add peas and fry an additional minute. Add approximately 6 cups of water to cover mixture and boil for 3 minutes. Cover and reduce heat. Simmer approximately 25 minutes or until all liquid is absorbed. Serves 6.

Reggae Curried Chicken
~ Jamaica ~

3 tablespoons vegetable oil
1 tablespoon curry powder
3 garlic cloves, minced
1½ pound chicken pieces
1 cup water
½ teaspoon dried thyme

1 large onion, chopped
½ teaspoon cumin
¼ teaspoon each salt and black pepper
1 medium peeled potato, cut into large cubes
¼ cup green and red bell peppers, seeded and chopped
1 teaspoon tomato purée (tomato paste)

2 green onions, chopped
¼ teaspoon celery salt
¼ teaspoon turmeric

In a large saucepan, sauté onions, peppers and garlic until onions are golden. Mix thyme, turmeric, cumin and celery salt in a bowl with just enough water from the 1 cup to make a smooth paste. Add to pepper and onion mixture. Rinse out bowl with more water, again taken from the 1 cup, and add to mixture. Save remaining water. Fry mixture over high heat, stirring frequently, until curry paste is very dry. Be sure to stir often so mixture does not burn. Add chicken and mix well. Over high heat, fry for a few minutes. Reduce to medium heat. Add remaining ingredients and stir well. Cook for 25 minutes in a covered pan until potatoes and chicken are done. Stir occasionally. Serves 4.

Rum Raisin Pigeon
~ St. John ~

8 pigeons, feathered and cleaned
1 tablespoon olive oil
1 teaspoon molasses
2 teaspoons arrowroot

4 tablespoons dark rum
1 onion, minced
⅔ cup chicken broth
dash salt and freshly ground pepper

4 tablespoons raisins
1 garlic clove, crushed
1 teaspoon hot pepper sauce
fresh cilantro, to garnish

Soak raisins in rum for 2 hours. Using a flame-proof casserole, cook pigeons in oil, browning evenly on all sides. Remove pigeons and set aside. Sauté garlic and onion in cooking oil for 10 minutes. Strain off rum from raisins, reserving raisins for garnishing. Place run in small pan. Set alight with a taper. When flames die down pour into casserole and blend in chicken stock, molasses, hot pepper sauce and seasoning. Place pigeons into mixture and cook for 20-30 minutes, covered, until done. In a small bowl, stir together arrowroot and water. Pour over casserole to thicken the sauce. Ladle onto pigeons occasionally while cooking for extra flavor. Garnish with cilantro and raisins. Serves 4.

Treasured Chicken
~ Tobago ~

1 (4 pounds) whole chicken
2 teaspoons cornstarch
¼ cup vegetable oil
¼ cup fresh thyme leaves
4 garlic cloves, minced

2 teaspoons water
½ cup dark rum
2 tablespoons fresh parsley, minced
1½ tablespoons fresh ginger, minced
3 chile peppers, seeded and minced

½ cup soy sauce
½ teaspoon dry mustard
¼ cup lime juice
1 medium onion

Slice chicken in half, clip the wings and remove bones around chicken breast. Place chicken in a roasting pan. In a food processor, add all ingredients except water and cornstarch. Process for 15 seconds or until a mashed mixture forms. Pour the mash over chicken and refrigerate for 2 hours. Preheat oven to 350°F. Cook chicken for 1 hour or until meat pulls easily from bones. Every 20 minutes, baste chicken with juices from the pan and turn pieces of chicken over. Mix water and cornstarch together and set aside. Place chicken on plates. In a skillet, add pan juices and mash. Add cornstarch mixture and simmer on medium heat, stirring frequently. Place the sauce in a bowl and serve. Serves 4.

Trinidad Pilau
~ Trinidad ~

2 pounds chicken pieces
5 garlic cloves, crushed
2 tablespoons soy sauce
1 hot pepper, seeded and chopped
3 cups rice, parboiled
½ cup green peas, cooked

1 onion, minced
8 celery leaves, finely chopped
2 tablespoons ketchup
5 tablespoons olive oil
4 tablespoons melted butter
½ cup carrots, chopped and cooked

1 scallion, minced
2 sprigs thyme, chopped
dash salt
2 tablespoons brown sugar
2½ cups water

In a large bowl, mix together onion, scallions, garlic, celery leaves, thyme, soy sauce, ketchup, hot pepper and salt. Marinate chicken with marinade mixture in a covered dish and refrigerate for at least 2 hours or overnight. At preparation time, drain off marinade and reserve. In a large saucepan, heat oil and sugar over a moderate heat until sugar is completely dissolved and syrup darkens. Add chicken pieces and brown evenly over a moderate high heat for 4-5 minutes. Pour in reserved marinade. Add a touch of water to bowl to rinse out marinade and save. Cook chicken for an additional 15 minutes, covered, at a moderate low heat. Add parboiled rice and melted butter to watered down marinade. Stir together. Then add chicken. Simmer until done, approximately 15-20 minutes. Add carrots and peas before serving. Serves 6-8.

Desserts

Antillean Carrot Cake
~ Aruba ~

6 large carrots (one pound)   *2 cups flour, sifted*   *3 eggs*
1 cup vegetable oil   *1½ cups brown sugar, firmly packed*   *1 teaspoon baking powder*
1 teaspoon cinnamon   *½ teaspoon baking soda*   *¼ teaspoon ground cloves*
¼ teaspoon ground ginger   *½ cup chopped walnuts*   *1 cup raisins*
1 cup glazed mixed fruit   *1 tablespoon confectioners' sugar*   *dash salt*

Preheat oven to 325ºF. Grate carrots finely to make 1½ cups. Sift flour into a bowl. Resift with baking soda, cinnamon, ginger, cloves and salt. Set aside. Beat eggs, brown sugar, chopped walnuts, raisins, glazed mixed fruit and oil. Blend liquid and dry ingredients together. Lightly butter a 10 inch baking pan and pour in cake mixture. Bake cake for 60 minutes or until done. After cake has cooled, place a doily on top and sprinkle confectioners' sugar over cake. Remove doily and a beautiful pattern remains on the cake. Serves 12 .

Arrowroot Custard
~ Grenadines ~

1 ounce arrowroot   *2 egg yolks, beaten*   *1 pint milk*
dash vanilla or almond essence   *1 ounce sugar*

With a little bit of cold milk, blend arrowroot to a smooth paste. Pour remaining milk in a pot and bring to a boil. When boiling, mix in the arrowroot paste. Remove pot from heat. Add sugar and return to stove. Cook for 3 minutes. Remove from heat and add in vanilla or almond essence and egg yolks. Stir. Pour into individual serving dishes and allow to cool. Serves 2.

Banana Gingersnaps
~ Jamaica ~

6 ripe bananas, chopped   *⅓ cup sugar*   *½ teaspoon ground ginger*
½ cup fresh pineapple juice   *¼ cup softened butter*   *½ cup shredded coconut*
16 crushed gingersnaps   *2 tablespoons light brown sugar*

Prepare a 350ºF oven and a greased 2 quart pan. Coat bananas with sugar and ginger in a bowl. Add in pineapple juice. Pour into pan. Mix together crushed gingersnaps, coconut, butter and light brown sugar. Layer on top of bananas. Bake until crispy, about 25-30 minutes. Serve from the oven. Makes 6 portions.

Banana-Rum Cake
~ Guadeloupe ~

2 large overripe bananas
7 ounces granulated sugar
2 tablespoons rum

3 eggs
8 ounces flour
½ cup water

2 ounces butter, melted
4 tablespoons sour cream
4 teaspoons lime juice

Preheat oven to 400°F. Mix together sour cream, bananas and rum. In another bowl, whisk sugar and eggs for 5 minutes. Add butter, flour and banana mixture and mix well. Pour into a greased 9 inch cake pan. Bake 40-45 minutes or until cake is done.

Rum syrup: Bring lime juice, water and sugar to a boil in a saucepan. Reduce heat and simmer 10 minutes to dissolve the sugar, stirring occasionally. Remove from heat and stir in rum. When the cake is done, turn it out onto a rack. Using a skewer, poke holes in cake then spoon on the rum syrup. Serves 4.

Banane Celeste
~ Martinique ~

3 tablespoons sugar
½ teaspoon ground cinnamon
6 firm bananas, peeled and halved

1½ pounds cream cheese, room temperature
2 tablespoons melted butter
3 tablespoons double cream

Preheat oven to 350°F. Blend cream cheese, cinnamon and sugar into a bowl until light and fluffy. Brown the banana halves, both sides, in melted butter. Remove the bananas and arrange six pieces in a layer at the bottom of a baking dish. Spoon half of the cream cheese mixture onto the bananas and spread evenly. Sandwich with another layer of bananas and then cream cheese. Top with the double cream. Bake until golden and top with a dash of cinnamon. Serves 3.

Barafie
~ Trinidad ~

1 cup almonds
1 cup rose water with ginger
¾ pound sugar

1 pound full-cream milk powder
1½ cans cream

1 cup cherries
¾ cup water

In a bowl, mix cream and powdered milk with fingers. Sift through a sieve. In a saucepan, boil water, sugar and rose water with ginger for 10 minutes. When mixture becomes syrup, remove the ginger. Mix into sifted mixture and press into a greased dish using the back of a spoon. Cut when cool and decorate with cherries and almonds. Serves 4.

Bolo di Rom
~ Curaçao ~

1 cup butter	1½ cups sugar	6 eggs
1½ cups all-purpose flour	¾ cup laraha, or bitter orange juice	1 cup yellow corn meal
2 teaspoon baking powder	¼ cup grated laraha, or bitter orange peel	
¼ cup rum	4 squares bittersweet chocolate	

Preheat oven to 350°F. Combine butter and sugar. Add eggs one at a time, beating mixture after each one. Blend in orange juice and peel. Sift and add flour, corn meal and baking powder. Add rum. Pour batter in a lightly grease 10 inch baking dish at least 2 inches deep. Bake for forty minutes. Melt chocolate over gently boiling water and whisk to remove any lumps. While cake is still warm, spread melted chocolate over top. Serve after icing has hardened. Serves 14.

Bridgetown Rum Cake
~ Barbados ~

/3 cup Barbados rum	1 lime, juiced	2 cups flour
1 cup unsalted butter	4 eggs	½ cup cornstarch
¼ teaspoon lime rind, grated	1½ cups light brown sugar	2 teaspoons baking powder

Preheat oven to 350°F. Grease a 9 inch loaf pan. In a bowl, cream the butter and slowly add sugar. Beat until light. Add in one egg at a time, beating the mixture after each egg. Add rind and lime juice and mix well. Sift all dry ingredients together and add to batter, stirring frequently. Then add rum, beat well and pour batter into the prepared pan. Bake for 1¼ hours, until brown on top. Insert a knife into the center. If the knife comes out clean, the cake in ready. Serve warm with rum raisin ice cream. Makes 1 cake.

Buñuelos de Viento
~ Cuba ~

½ cup water	1 tablespoon butter	½ teaspoon salt
½ cup all-purpose flour	½ teaspoon grated citrus zest or cinnamon	
2 eggs	3 cups vegetable, oil for frying	

Lime Syrup: 2 cups water	1 cup sugar	¼ teaspoon lime zest, grated

Buñuelos: Blend water, salt, spice flavoring and butter together into a pan on moderate heat and boil. Reduce to low and stir in flour until smooth, allowing to thicken. At a very low heat, beat in eggs gradually. Set aside. Heat oil for frying in a separate pan at a high temperature. Drop dough by the tablespoonful into hot oil. Fry until dough becomes golden and puffed. Drain well on paper towels. Serve warm.

Lime syrup: Bring water and sugar to a boil on high heat. Reduce down to medium heat and add grated zest. Cook for 20 minutes until syrup forms. Lightly drizzle buñuelos with syrup. Serves 4-6.

Calypso Banana-Ginger Ice Cream
~ Trinidad ~

½ cup light brown sugar
3 ripe bananas, mashed
2 tablespoons ginger syrup

1 (16 ounce) can evaporated milk, chilled
ginger syrup, to garnish
4 ounces preserved ginger, chopped

Turn freezer setting to high. Whisk evaporated milk until thickened. Add sugar. Whisk in bananas and ginger syrup. Spoon in chopped ginger. Put in a covered freezer container and freeze for three hours. Mash with fork and return to freezer for two more hours. Repeat procedure and finish freezing for another 3 hours. Let stand at room temperature for 20 minutes before serving. Adorn with ginger syrup. Serves 8.

_____

Captain Morgan's Rum Cake
~ Cayman Islands ~

3 cups flour
dash salt
1 teaspoon vanilla extract
I cup dark rum
rum for added flavor

2 teaspoons baking powder
1½ cups butter, softened
3 eggs
1 cup heavy cream
1 egg yolk

1 teaspoon baking soda
1½ cups sugar
1 tablespoon lemon zest
confectioners' sugar

Prepare a 350°F oven. Butter and flour a 10 cup tube pan. Sift together dry ingredients. Place in a separate bowl. Beat sugar and butter until creamy and light. Mix in vanilla, beaten eggs and egg yolk. Beat in rum and lemon zest. Slowly add, alternately, dry ingredients and butter cream. Pour batter into prepared pan and bake for about an hour. Cool and arrange on a plate. Sprinkle with rum and shower with confectioners' sugar.

_____

Carambola Upside Down Delight
~ Florida Keys ~

3-4 star fruits, sliced (carambola)
½ cup softened butter
1½ cups all-purpose flour
½ cup milk

⅔ cup dark brown sugar
1 cup sugar
1½ teaspoons baking powder
1 teaspoon vanilla extract

2 juiced passion fruit
2 eggs
dash salt
1 teaspoon almond extract

Prepare a 350° F oven. Grease a 9 inch cake pan. Layer sliced star fruit generously on bottom of pan. Blend melted butter, brown sugar and passion fruit juice into a syrup mixture. Pour into cake pan, lifting slices to allow syrup to coat bottom as well as fruit. Set to the side. Cream softened butter and sugar together. Add in beaten eggs and mix well. Sift together dry ingredients. Add dry portions to creamed butter while pouring in alternate parts of milk. Swirl in extract flavorings. Pour batter into cake pan and bake for about 30 minutes. Allow to cool for 5 minutes before flipping out on to a serving platter. Serves 8.

Château (Chocolate Trifle)
~ Aruba ~

1½ cups rich cream	4 ounces unsweetened baking chocolate	2 cups butter
¼ cup slivered almonds	3½ cups confectioners' sugar, sifted	4 eggs
1 teaspoon vanilla	6 maraschino cherries	

Pan levi: 4 eggs, beaten	1 cup sugar	2½ cups flour
¼ teaspoon mace	¼ teaspoon vanilla	dash salt

Pan levi: Preheat oven to 350°F. In a bowl, gently beat eggs until slightly foamy. Stir in sugar, salt, vanilla and mace. Blend flour in slowly until well mixed. Place batter by tablespoonfuls on a lightly greased cookie sheet. Form batter into a peaked mound, about 2 inches in diameter. Bake for 10-15 minutes or until edges are golden. Place pan levi on a cooling rack for about 10 minutes.

Melt chocolate over gently boiling water and whisk to remove any lumps. Incorporate cream a bit at a time. Whisk until smooth. Chill. Beat butter until light and creamy. Add sugar and beat in eggs one at a time. Add vanilla. Blend in chilled mixture. In a large serving bowl, place six pan levi on the bottom. Cover with a layers of chocolate. Add a second layer of pan levi. Press cookies into chocolate. Repeat until bowl is full. Top with a layer of chocolate. Garnish with cut cherries and almonds. Chill overnight and serve chilled. Serves 24.

Christmas Cake
~ Guyana ~

2 cups flour	2 pounds mixed raisins, pitted prunes and currants	
1 teaspoon ground allspice	6 eggs	1 cup butter
2 fifths of rum (2 bottles)	¼ cup mixed fruit peel	2¼ cups dark brown sugar
¼ teaspoon baking powder	½ cup walnuts, chopped	

In a food processor grind currants, raisins and prunes until a paste forms. Pour 1 bottle of rum over the ground fruit paste. Allow mixture to soak for 24-36 hours. Thoroughly grease two 8 inch cake pans. Preheat oven to 300°F. In a pan, blend 1½ cups of brown sugar, eggs and butter. Add walnuts and mixed peel to the fruit mixture and stir well. Caramelize the rest of the brown sugar. Let cool slightly and add ½ cup of rum, then add to fruit and peel mixture. Stir in the dry ingredients a little at a time until a batter forms. If batter is too thick, add more rum. Pour batter in baking pans. Bake for 1¼ hours. Stick a toothpick in center to test for doneness. If toothpick comes out clean, the cake will be too dry. Pour a generous amount of rum over each cake. As cake cools down, continue to soak with rum. Cakes may be covered with almond paste or decorated with icing. Makes 2 cakes.

Clafoutis aux Bananas Tropicale
~ Martinique ~

3 halved bananas, lengthwise	½ cup shredded coconut, sweet	3 beaten eggs
¼ cup dark rum	1 cup half and half cream	½ cup sugar
½ cup all-purpose flour	dash nutmeg	

Prepare a 10 inch greased pie pan and oven at 375°F. Place banana halves into pan and sprinkle with coconut. Blend together remaining ingredients on high speed. Pour creamed mixture over bananas and bake until golden brown, about 45 minutes. Serves 4.

Cocada (Coconut Candy)
~ Aruba ~

1 pound brown sugar   *1 pound freshly grated coconut*   *1 cup water*
½ lime, juiced

Combine in a saucepan the sugar and water. Simmer until thick syrup forms. In a cup of cold water, drop a little boiling syrup. When syrup can be made into a soft ball with fingers, remove from heat. Stir in coconut and lime juice. Drop by desired size onto parchment paper to cool. Makes 3 cups.

Coconut Cake
~ Aruba ~

1 cup butter   *2 cups sugar*   *6 eggs*
2 cups flour   *2 cups grated coconut*   *1 teaspoon vanilla*

Preheat oven to 300°F. Combine butter and sugar. Add eggs one at a time, beat well after each one. Sift flour and add to mixture. Add coconut and vanilla. Lightly grease a deep 10 inch cake pan and dust with flour. Spread batter evenly in pan and bake at 300°F for one hour. Bake an additional 20 minutes at 200°F. Serves 12.

Coconut Ice Cream
~ Cuba ~

1 cup coconut milk   *1 cup milk*   *1 cup sugar*
3 tablespoons cornstarch   *2 tablespoons coconut, grated*   *¼ teaspoon salt*
2 egg whites, beaten to peaks

In a saucepan, combine coconut milk and half of the milk. Mix together the other portion of milk with cornstarch and add into pan with salt and sugar. Cook while stirring constantly over a moderate low heat until mixture forms a custard texture. Blend in coconut and allow to cool. Pour into a covered freezer container and set in freezer. Remove when partially frozen. In a bowl, blend with egg whites until creamy. Place back into freezer for 3 hours. Remove and beat until smooth. Place into freezer again until frozen. Serves 4.

Coconut Pudding
~ Dominica ~

1 (14 ounce) can coconut milk   *2 tablespoons butter*   *1 lime rind, grated*
2 eggs, separated   *1½ cups fresh white bread crumbs*   *¼ cup confectioners' sugar*
3-4 tablespoons guava jelly, warmed   *shredded lime rind for garnishing*

Prepare a baking pan coated with butter. Preheat oven to 350°F. In a pan, bring butter, coconut milk and grated lime to a boil. Reserve to the side. Whisk together yolks and half of the sugar. Add in coconut blend. Layer breadcrumbs in prepared dish. Strain coconut blend over the breadcrumbs and allow to soak in for 20 minutes. Bake pudding until firm, about 30 minutes. When done, remove from the oven and spread guava jelly over the top of the pudding. Beat and stiffen egg whites. Whisk the last of the sugar into egg whites. Pile on top of pudding. Bake meringue until light golden, about 10-15 minutes. Serves 4.

Crema di Sorsaka (Soursop Bavarian Cream)
~ Aruba ~

2 medium soursaps
¼ cup cold water
1 cup heavy cream

2 tablespoons gelatin
½ cup sugar

1¾ cup light cream
dash salt

Peel and seed soursop, then run pulp through a sieve. Divide into two equal portions. Soak gelatin in cold water. Scald cream in a saucepan. Add sugar and salt stirring until mixture dissolves. Blend in gelatin. Stir in one portion of soursap. Add sugar to taste to the second portion. Refrigerate for later use. Chill gelatin mixture until it begins to thicken. Whisk until fluffy. Beat heavy cream until stiff. Fold into gelatin mixture. Place pudding in serving dish and chill. Just before serving, spoon remaining soursap over pudding. Serves 6.

―――――――――――

Down Island Coconut Pudding
~ Barbados ~

4 egg yolks
5 tablespoons butter
1 tablespoon vanilla extract
2 cups fresh breadcrumbs

2 cups grated fresh or dried unsweetened coconut
2 tablespoons rum
1 cup coconut milk

1 cup milk
6 tablespoons brown sugar

Preheat oven to 350ºF. Thoroughly mix all ingredients together in a large bowl. Pour mixture into an ovenproof dish. Bake for 1 hour. Serve warm. Serves 4-6.

―――――――――――

Extravagant Guanabana Soufflé
~ Cuba ~

Soufflé: 1 (14 ounce) package frozen guanabana (soursop) purée
1 cup heavy cream
2 tablespoons granulated sugar

½ cup powdered sugar
2 tablespoons all-purpose flour, sifted

1 tablespoon lime, juiced
4 extra large eggs, separated

Lime Butter: ⅓ cup sugar
¼ cup fresh lime juice

4 tablespoons butter, melted
¼ cup heavy cream

1 extra large egg, beaten

Soufflé: Simmer soursop for 10 minutes, to thaw and remove excess moisture, stirring constantly. When 1¼ cups remain, add lime juice and set aside to cool. Preheat oven to 350ºF. Lightly butter 4 ounce (½ cup) soufflé molds. Dust with granulated sugar. In a saucepan, bring the cream to a boil, whisking often. Remove from heat. In a mixing bowl, sift together powdered sugar and flour. Blend in beaten egg yolks. Pour some hot cream into the egg and flour mix, and combine well. Then, introduce mixture into the saucepan of hot cream. On medium heat, whisk these ingredients until thick. Transfer ingredients to a large bowl and include guanabana and lime mix. Beat egg whites until stiff while slowly adding in sugar. Spoon into the total fruit mixture. Pour the filling into the soufflé molds, level to the top. Place soufflé molds in a pan with warm water that reaches half way up the sides. Place pan in the middle of the oven. Bake for 35 minutes. Sprinkle with powdered sugar.

Lime Butter: Melt butter in double boiler. Beat sugar and egg together in a small bowl. Whisk into the melted butter. Remove top half of boiler from heat and whisk in lime and cream. Keep warm for

Flan de Piña
~ Puerto Rico ~

2 cups pineapple juice   1 cup sugar   1 tablespoon brandy
8 eggs, beaten

Preheat oven to 350°F and grease a round baking dish. Pour pineapple juice and sugar in a saucepan and bring to a boil. Then simmer to a thick syrup and cool. Beat syrup and brandy into beaten eggs. Pour mixture into greased baking dish. Place dish with mixture into a roasting pan. Fill roasting pan with hot water to halfway up the outside of the baking dish. Bake for about an hour, until knife inserted in center comes out dry. Remove and chill. Serves 6.

Frozen Passion
~ Florida Keys ~

6-8 ripe passion fruits   ½ cup sugar   3 extra large egg yolks
2 extra large egg whites   ½ cup heavy cream, chilled

Halve the passion fruits, remove seeds and juice (⅔ cup required). The shells of the fruits are to be used in presentation as a container. Cut a thin slice off the bottom of each shell to level it. Wrap the sides with masking tape for a clean presentation. Cut 12 strips of parchment paper, each (6x2½ inches). Wrap around the top rim of each shell allowing for 1 inch to stand above the shell, like a collar, then tape to secure. Place each shell into one well of a muffin tin. Blend together sugar, egg yolks and ⅓ of a cup of passion fruit juice, strained. Like a double boiler, place bowl over a pan of boiling water and whisk well to a 160°F. Remove from heat and continue to whisk until color is pale yellow and liquid has cooled. Whip the cream into soft peaks and fold in passion fruit blend. Beat egg whites until stiff and spoon into creamy fruit blend. Place approximately ¼ cup of the mix into each passion fruit shell and freeze. Before serving remove parchment and anchor 2-3 filled passion shells into a bed of ice per person. Decorate with edible flowers and color ice with any remaining juice. Serves 4.

Fruity Key Lime Muffins
~ Florida Keys ~

2 large ripe bananas, mashed   1 cup coconut flakes   ½ cup butter, softened
1 cup sugar   1 egg   1 teaspoon Key lime zest
½ cup buttermilk   2¼ cups all-purpose flour   2 teaspoons baking powder
½ teaspoon baking soda   ½ teaspoon salt   ¼ teaspoon nutmeg

Preheat oven to 350°F. Grease a 12 inch muffin pan. Cream butter and sugar with an electric mixer in a large bowl. Add buttermilk and egg and beat until fluffy. Add lemon zest and bananas. Beat to combine. Combine flour, baking powder, baking soda, nutmeg and salt. Gradually add dry ingredients to mixture. Beat after each addition to completely blend. Spoon into muffin pan ¾ full. Bake for 25-30 minutes. Remove pan and allow to cool on wire rack. Makes 12 muffins.

Gâteau de Patate
~ Haiti ~

2½ ounces butter, softened
1 large ripe banana
8 ounces sugar
¼ teaspoon vanilla essence
1½ ounces raisins

2 pounds sweet potatoes, peeled and quartered
3 eggs
6 tablespoons evaporated milk
¼ teaspoon ground cinnamon

6 ounces dark corn syrup
6 tablespoons coconut milk
¼ teaspoon ground nutmeg

Preheat oven to 350°F. Cream a cake pan with ½ ounce of butter. Boil sweet potatoes until soft. Drain and blend with bananas in a mixer. Add remaining ingredients and mix well. Pour into prepared cake pan and bake for 1½ hours. Allow to cool for 10 minutes and turn out on a wire rack to completely cool. Serve with Coquimol (see page: 19).

Ginger Cake
~ Cayman Islands ~

2 cups self-rising flour
¾ cup brown sugar, dark
2 eggs, beaten

1 tablespoon fresh ground ginger
¼ teaspoon freshly ground nutmeg
1½ tablespoons corn syrup

½ teaspoon baking soda
½ cup butter, melted
1½ tablespoons milk

Topping: 6 pieces candied ginger, quartered
4 teaspoons ginger syrup
1 fresh lemon, juiced

1 cup confectioners' sugar

Prepare a 325°F oven. Grease and line a 7 inch cake square pan. Sift together dry ingredients. Add in butter and dark brown sugar separately. Whisk together eggs, corn syrup and milk. Beat into dry ingredient mixture until a smooth batter is achieved. Pour into prepared pan and bake for 45-50 minutes until firm in the middle. Allow to cool.

Topping: Place ginger pieces on top of cake in desired pattern. Sift the confectioners' sugar into a small bowl. Pour in ginger syrup and lemon juice and beat until smooth. Swirl onto cake using a pastry funnel. Cover and refrigerate for 24 hours. Serves 12.

Grenada Bread Pudding
~ Grenada ~

3 large eggs, well beaten
1½ teaspoons vanilla extract
2 cups milk

6 ounces nutmeg syrup (Morne Delice, an island specialty)
1¼ teaspoons nutmeg
5 cups bread, cubed

½ cup grenadine liqueur
½ cup raisins

In a large bowl, blend together all ingredients except bread and raisins. Layer the bread cubes in a greased bread pan. Spoon the raisins and liquid mix over the bread pieces and allow to soak in for about 45 minutes. Occasionally tap the ingredients together for more saturation. Preheat a 350°F oven and bake for around 40 minutes. Serve with Concord cream.

Guava Sorbet
~ Dominican Republic ~

¼ cup water
¼ cup superfine sugar (caster)

2 teaspoons unflavored gelatin
3 tablespoons white rum

2 cups pink guavas, puréed

Add gelatin to water in a baker's bowl. Over a low heat, allow to dissolve. Let cool. Mix into puréed guava. Stir in rum and sugar. Lightly freeze in a covered container. Beat sorbet and then return to freezer until solid. Place in refrigerator for 20 minutes to soften before serving. Serves 4.

———————————

Hot Cross Easter Buns
~ Barbados ~

1 cup milk
3 teaspoons baking powder
1½ cups brown sugar
1 tablespoon cinnamon

3 cups flour
¼ cup orange and lemon peel
1 cup raisins

1 cup icing sugar
2 eggs
1 tablespoon browning

Preheat oven to 350ºF. In a large bowl, mix all ingredients except icing sugar. Pour into well-greased and floured bun pans. Bake until raised, browned and cooked through. Glaze with a little icing sugar melted in water. When cool, mix water and icing sugar into a thick consistency. Use icing to make the sign of a cross on each bun. Makes 15 buns.

———————————

Island Mango Sorbet
~ Islamorada, Florida Keys ~

1 teaspoon Key lime juice
1 cup water

2 large ripe mangoes, peeled and cut from the pit
1 cup sugar

Purée mango pieces and strain to remove fibers. Set aside. In a small saucepan over medium high heat, combine sugar, water and Key lime juice. Simmer and stir constantly for 5 minutes. Remove from heat and let cool. Combine syrup with mango purée in a large mixing bowl. Pour the mixture into an ice cream machine and freeze according to manufacturer's directions. Makes 2 pints.

———————————

Jelabi
~ Guyana ~

2 cups all-purpose flour
¼ teaspoon saffron, powdered
¼ teaspoon cardamom, ground

¼ cup unflavored yogurt
1¾ cups water, room temperature
vegetable oil, for frying

1¼ cups warm water
1¼ cups sugar

Make a batter out of yogurt, flour and warm water. Add in saffron. Cover with a cloth and leave overnight to set mixture. Boil together sugar, water and cardamom. Reduce to a lower heat and cook until a thick syrup. Smooth out yogurt batter, beating well. Over a moderate high heat, prepare oil for frying. Pour the batter through a funnel while spilling out into the pan in a circular motion, forming a 4-5 inch diameter coil. Stop the batter flow and cook each jelabi until golden brown on each side. Drain on a paper towel. Dip the jelabi evenly into the cardamom syrup. Serve them hot in stacks. Makes 12-14.

Kesio
~ Curaçao ~

1 cup sugar
2 teaspoons vanilla extract
4 maraschino cherries

dash salt
2 cups milk, warmed
light rum

5 eggs, beaten
3 ounces water

Prepare a 350°F oven and grease a 6 inch glass baking dish with butter. Portion half the sugar into a pan and dissolve over a low heat until a caramel forms. Spoon into baking dish and coat the inside. Add sugar, salt and vanilla to beaten eggs. Slowly blend in milk. Pour into coated baking dish. Place dish in a roasting pan with 1 inch of hot water. Bake for 1 hour until firm, then allow to cool. Turn out onto a decorative serving platter and top with cherries. Flambé using a tablespoon of rum on each serving. Set alight for 10 seconds and blow out. Serves 4-6.

Key Largo Summer Drop Cookies
~ Key Largo, Florida Keys ~

1 stick soft butter
1 cup light brown sugar
1½ cups white flour
¾ cup shredded coconut

¾ cup dehydrated mango, finely cut
½ cup dehydrated pineapple, finely cut
½ teaspoon baking powder
½ cup chopped macadamia nuts

boiled water
1 egg, well beaten
dash salt

Prepare 350°F oven. Soak dehydrated fruits in a small amount of boiled water for 1 minute. Drain off water and place fruit into a mixing bowl. Add all ingredients together and blend well. Drop well rounded tablespoons of cookie dough onto a greased and floured baking pan. Bake until golden. Allow to cool and enjoy. Makes 48 cookies.

Key Lime-Coconut Pie
~ Florida Keys ~

1¼ cups coconut milk
2 large eggs, separated

3-4 Key limes, juiced and rind grated
¾ cup superfine sugar

¼ cup cornstarch

Pastry: 1½ cups all-purpose flour
1 teaspoon superfine sugar

dash salt
1 egg yolk

⅓ cup butter

Prepare a 375°F oven and set aside an 8 inch quiche pan.

Pastry: Sift together dry ingredients. Rub butter into sifted ingredients until the texture crumbles. Add in sugar, egg yolk and cold water gradually to create a firm dough. On a floured surface, roll out dough. Drape over quiche pan and line the form. Trim edges. Chill for 30 minutes. Line pie shell with parchment paper and dry beans. Bake about 15 minutes. Remove parchment liner and beans. Finish baking for an additional 5-10 minutes until golden. Reduce oven temperature to 325°F.

Meringue Filling: In a saucepan, slowly add the cornstarch and coconut milk. Stir constantly until mixture begins to boil. Cook for about 3 minutes more, until thickened, while continuing to stir. Remove from heat. Add in Key lime juice, rind, egg yolks and ¼ cup of sugar. Pour into pastry shell. Stiffen egg whites and whisk in sugar. Gently swirl egg whites over pie with a palette knife. Bake 10-15 minutes more until top is golden. Garnish with grated Key lime rind. Serves 6.

Key West Bight Meringuettes
~ Key West, Florida Keys ~

3 separated eggs
1 cup sugar
1 cup whipped heavy cream

pinch of salt
1½ teaspoons grated Key lime rind

¼ cup cream of tartar
4 tablespoons Key lime juice

Prepare a "slow" oven at 275°F.

Meringue: Beat egg whites until stiff. Add in salt and cream of tartar and stiffen again. Slowly add ¾ cup of sugar and beat until very firm. On a baking sheet covered with heavy brown paper, mound meringue fluff about 6 inches round and 3 inches high. Depress the center of each mound to form a (crater) for filling.

Filling: Beat egg yolks and add in the last ¼ cup of sugar along with Key lime juice. Cook in a double boiler, stirring until thickened. Add in grated Key lime. Remove and chill. Swirl whipped cream into chilled lime filling. Spoon filling into formed meringue shell. Chill again for at least 6 more hours before serving. Serves 6.

Keys-Style Bananas Flambé
~ Key Largo, Florida Keys ~

2 tablespoons butter
¼ cup dark rum
¼ cup crème de banana
2 tablespoons brown sugar

1 pint vanilla or chocolate ice cream or frozen yogurt
4 bananas, peeled and sliced crosswise
¼ teaspoon ground cinnamon

In a large skillet, add brown sugar and butter. Cook over medium heat until it forms a syrup. Add cinnamon and banana slices and sauté 3 minutes. Gently turn slices to coat with the syrup. Pour in the rum and crème de banana. Touch a match to the liqueur, let flame subside and cook for 1 minute. Scoop the ice cream into bowls and top with bananas. Serves 4.

Kumquat Treats
~ Florida Keys ~

10 kumquats
⅔ cup sugar
⅓ cup orange juice

Cover kumquats with water in a saucepan. Bring to a boil. Drain. Place kumquats in a bowl with ice water and cool. Drain and trim off each end. Mix sugar and orange juice together and bring to a boil in a saucepan. Reduce to simmer, add fruit and cook for about 50-60 minutes, stirring often to prevent sticking. Place on parchment paper and let stand until cooled into candy treats.

Lychee Delight
~ Martinique ~

1 (20 ounce) can lychees
¼ cup shredded coconut

½ gallon French vanilla ice cream
¼ cup chopped nuts

1 tablespoon almond extract

Drain lychees and reserve juice. Cut lychees into halves and add 3 tablespoons drained juice. Add lychees, almond extract, coconut and nuts to the softened ice cream. Mix well and refreeze. Serves 12.

Mama's Secret Recipe Cookies
~ Bahamas ~

1 tablespoon dark rum
2 eggs
½ teaspoon salt
¼ teaspoon freshly grated nutmeg
½ cup macadamia or cashew nuts, unsalted and chopped

½ cup unsalted butter, softened
2 cups all-purpose flour
1 teaspoon cinnamon, ground
1 cup raisins, chopped

1 cup brown sugar
1 teaspoon baking powder
¼ teaspoon cloves, ground
1 cup dates, chopped

Prepare a 350°F oven and greased cookie sheets. In a mixing bowl, blend together rum, butter and brown sugar until smooth. Sift together dry ingredients and mix into rum butter. Add dates, raisins and nuts. Using a generous tablespoon measure, arrange cookie dough on baking sheets. Place in oven for about 10 minutes, until golden brown. Makes 4 dozen.

Mango Cheesecake
~ Virgin Islands ~

8 slices mango
4 tablespoons ripe mango pulp
4 tablespoons brown sugar
¼ cup sugar
¼ pint sour cream

½ pound graham crackers, crushed
2½ tablespoons butter, melted
1 pound soft cream cheese
1 teaspoon ground cinnamon
dash salt

2 eggs, well beaten
1 teaspoon lime juice
½ teaspoon vanilla essence
¼ teaspoon ground nutmeg

Preheat oven to 375°F. In a large bowl, mix 2 tablespoons of brown sugar, butter and crushed crackers. Firmly press into an 8 inch pie pan, form and refrigerate. In a separate bowl, beat eggs, lime juice, sugar, salt and cream cheese together, then mix in mango pulp. Remove pie crust from refrigerator and pour in filling. Bake for 20 minutes. Take out of oven and spread ½ of the cinnamon over cheesecake, and allow to cool. In another bowl, beat the sour cream. Add nutmeg, remaining brown sugar and vanilla. Mix well. Mix in the mango slices. Pour over cheesecake and bake 5 minutes. Remove from oven, sprinkle rest of cinnamon over the top and allow to cool. Refrigerate for 8 hours before serving. Extra mango can be used as decoration. Serves 6-8.

Mango Ice Cream
~ St. Lucia ~

1 pound ripe mango pulp
½ teaspoon lime juice

1 cup heavy cream
1 cup castor sugar, superfine

8 eggs, separated

Whisk egg whites until stiff. Add in sugar and whisk until fluffy. In a separate bowl, whisk cream until firm. Beat the egg yolks then whisk into egg whites. Add lime juice, mango and cream, then pour mixture into an ice cream tub and put in freezer for 2 hours. Remove and mix in blender or by hand. Pour into ice cream tub and freeze. Serves 4.

Mango Islander Mousse
~ Key West, Florida Keys ~

1 package orange gelatin
½ cups boiling water
8 ounces heavy whipping cream

8 ounce package cream cheese, softened to room temperature
1 cup mango, peeled, cut into chunks and puréed
½ cup sugar

Combine gelatin and water. Mix in sugar until dissolved. Place in refrigerator. Beat whipped cream in a bowl until almost stiff. Refrigerate. Blend mango purée and softened cream cheese until smooth. When gelatin is cooled and has not yet stiffened, whisk gelatin into whipped cream. Fold in mango cream cheese mixture. Blend gently until smooth. Pour into mold and chill. Serves 6.

Mango Upside-Down Delight
~ Key West, Florida Keys ~

2 tablespoons Key lime juice
¼ cup brown sugar
1 egg
2 teaspoons baking powder

2 cups peeled and sliced ripe mangoes
¼ cup shortening
½ cup milk
¼ teaspoon salt

1 tablespoon margarine
¾ cup sugar
1¼ cups flour

Marinate mangoes for 15 minutes with Key lime juice. Melt margarine in 8 inch round pan (Do not use iron skillet as mangoes will darken). Add brown sugar and cover with mango slices. For cake batter, cream shortening and add beaten egg. Sift dry ingredients and add alternately with milk. Pour over mangoes and bake 50-60 minutes at 375°F. When done, turn upside down and serve.

Marzipan-Orange Meringues
~ Florida Keys ~

8 ounces almond paste (marzipan)
pinch cream of tartar

4 teaspoons orange rind, grated
½ cup sugar, superfine

2 egg whites
sugar for topping

Prepare a 250°F oven and 2 baking sheets, greased and floured. Press together marzipan and grated orange evenly. Cut in half and roll out a 15 inch strip. Divide into ¾ inch pieces and form a tiny ball with each one. Beat egg whites along with cream of tartar until stiff. On high speed, beat in portions of sugar until very stiff and well blended. Coat each orange marzipan, like a small snowball, and gently arrange on baking sheet. Lightly shower each ball with a layer of sugar and place in oven for 55-60 minutes. Makes 3 dozen.

Orange Cake
~ Antigua ~

¾ cup melted sweet butter
2 cups white flour
dash salt

¾ cup sugar, or less to taste
2 teaspoons fresh orange rind, ground
½ cup orange juice

3 eggs, blended
1 tablespoon baking powder

Grease a loaf pan (9x5 inch) and preheat oven to 350°F. Mix sugar and butter into a cream. Add in beaten eggs individually. Blend in grated orange rind. Combine dry ingredients of sifted flour, baking powder and salt. Gently blend dry ingredients and orange juice, one at a time, into batter. Pour into butter greased loaf pan. Bake approximately 45-60 minutes. When dry in middle, remove from oven and air on baker's shelf to cool.

Papa's Favorite Potato Pie
~ U.S. Virgin Islands ~

2 eggs, beaten
⅓ cup light brown sugar

2¼ cups sweet potato, diced
1 tablespoon mixed spice

2 cups evaporated milk

Pastry: 1½ cups all-purpose flour
1 teaspoon superfine sugar

dash salt
cold water

⅓ cup butter
1 egg yolk

Prepare a 375ºF oven. Boil sweet potatoes for 10 minutes and drain. Mash well and set aside to cool.

Pastry: Sift salt and flour into a bowl. Crumble dry ingredients with butter. Add in sugar egg yolk, and enough cold water to form a dough consistency. Roll out on to a floured surface. Press into a round 9 inch quiche pan and chill about 30 minutes. Line pastry shell with baking parchment and dry beans to preheat and form crust. Bake for about 10 minutes. Remove parchment and beans to lightly golden shell, baking 5 more minutes. In a mixing bowl combine sweet potatoes, eggs, sugar, milk and spices. Pour filling into quiche shell and bake for 30 minutes. Turn down heat to 350°F and bake an additional 10 minutes until just firm. May be served hot or cold. Sift a light layer of confectioners' sugar to garnish. Serves 8.

Papaya Ice Cream
~ Jamaica ~

4 tablespoons arrowroot powder
2 pints milk

1 ripe papaya, peeled, seeded, and blended
¼ pint evaporated milk

4 ounces cane sugar

Mix a little of the milk and the arrowroot. In a pan, heat the rest of the milk until boiling. Slowly stir in arrowroot. Cook until thick. Remove from heat and allow to cool. Add sugar and evaporated milk. Stir until sugar has dissolved completely. Add papaya purée and pour into freezer container. After 1 hour, remove from freezer and beat with fork. Put back in freezer and repeat process after another hour. Repeat two more times reducing elapsed time to 30 minutes each. Freeze again and serve topped with papaya and fruit of your choice. Serves 4.

Passion Fruit Crème
~ St.Nevis ~

1 teaspoon passion fruit juice
4 egg yolks
dash cherry syrup

1 cup sugar
2 whole eggs

1 cup milk
1 sprig mint

Preheat oven to 250°F. Beat eggs, yolks and sugar in a bowl. In a saucepan, warm juice and milk together. Pour in eggs and sugar mixture. Stir continuously with wooden spoon. Strain and pour into 4 small custard dishes. In a roasting pan ⅔ full of hot water, place custard dishes. Bake 20 minutes, making sure water does not boil. If necessary, add cold water. After 20 minutes, check crème by inserting a knife. If knife comes out clean, it's ready. Allow to cool, then refrigerate for at least 6 hours. Garnish with sprig of mint and passion fruit syrup. Serves 4.

———————————————

Pasteles
~ Cuba ~

3 cups all-purpose flour
½ teaspoon ground cinnamon
6 pink guavas, peeled, seeded, sliced
½ cup milk

1¼ teaspoons salt
1 cup margarine, cut into small cubes
1 cup water
1 tablespoon milk

¼ teaspoon baking powder
1 tablespoon butter
½ cup sugar

Sift dry ingredients together. Slowly add in shortening until mixture it becomes a lumpy consistency. Blend in ½ cup milk until the dough sticks together. If more liquid is needed, add water by the tablespoonful. Knead for 1 minute and refrigerate. In a saucepan, add remainder of ingredients except the 1 tablespoon of milk and boil on high, stirring often. Cool when only a small amount of liquid remains and guava is still intact. Roll out pastry into a 9 inch square. Slice into 3 inch squares. Place 1-2 tablespoons of guava filling onto each square. Fold in half to create a rectangle and press edges together and seal. Brush milk on top of pasteles. Prepare a 350°F oven and bake for about 25-35 minutes, until golden. Cool and serve. Makes 9.

———————————————

Pineapple Pie
~ Antigua ~

1 cup pineapple juice
5 slices pineapple, chopped
4 egg yolks

1 cup icing sugar
1 cup milk
⅓ cup flour

9 inch pie crust
6 egg whites
1 cup sugar

Preheat oven to 300°F. Place pie crust in oven until brown. In a saucepan, boil juice and milk. In a large bowl, mix egg yolks, flour and sugar, then pour in juice and milk. Stir well, avoiding lumps. Pour mixture into saucepan and simmer on low heat. Stir continuously with wooden spoon until cream becomes thick consistency. Do not allow cream to boil. Add in pineapple chunks. Remove from heat. Cool for 5 minutes and pour into piecrust. Allow to cool completely.

Meringue: Beat egg whites until fluffy and mix in sugar slowly. Remove with a spatula. Cover pie with meringue. Bake under broiler until golden. Top with cherry. Serves 4-6.

Quesillo (Crème Caramel)
~ Dominican Republic ~

4 eggs, separated   8 tablespoons sugar   4 tablespoons water
dash salt   2 cups hot milk

In a saucepan, caramelize the sugar. When brown, add water and mix. Remove from heat and pour into cake mold. Preheat oven to 325°F. Beat egg whites and yolks separately. Then add yolks to whites slowly. Mix in sugar, salt and milk. Pour into caramelize mold. Place the mold in a pan of water and bake for 45 minutes. Bake until an inserted knife comes out clean. Allow to cool before turning out of the mold. Serves 4.

Rum and Raisin Fudge
~ Jamaica ~

½ cup water   1 cup sweetened condensed milk   2 cups dark brown sugar
1 tablespoon light or dark rum   ½ cup seedless raisins, minced   ¼ cup melted butter
1 teaspoon vanilla extract

Prepare a buttered 6 inch square pan. Boil water, reduce heat and add in sugar. When sugar is dissolved, allow to thicken and remove from heat. Stir in sweetened milk over a moderate low heat until temperature reaches an ideal 245°F on a candy thermometer. Remove from stove and mix together with butter, raisins, rum and vanilla. Beat until thick, approximately 4 minutes. Pour mixture into buttered pan and allow to cool. Serve cut in squares. Makes 20 pieces.

Rum Banana Brulée
~ British Virgin Islands ~

1 cup coconut cream   1¾ cups heavy cream   1 vanilla pod, split
6 egg yolks, whisked   ½ cup superfine sugar   2 small bananas, sliced
4 tablespoons dark rum   6 tablespoons brown sugar   fresh mint leaves, to garnish

Prepare a 325°F oven. Slowly heat cream, vanilla beans and coconut cream until almost boiling. Do not boil. In a side bowl, whisk egg yolks and superfine sugar until creamy. Stir vanilla coconut cream into egg mixture. Fashion a double boiler and stir mixture until it has a custard texture. Soak banana slices with rum in a side dish. Place banana slices in 6 custard dishes and pour the coconut custard on top. Arrange dishes in a roasting pan with a layer of water halfway up dishes. Bake for 5 minutes until firm. Cool and refrigerate overnight. Cool and set for 3-4 hours. Before presentation, preheat broiler. Layer custard dishes with brown sugar and caramelize for 3 minutes. Serves 6.

Soursop Ice Cream
~ U.S. Virgin Islands ~

3 cups soursop pulp   1 cup sweetened condensed milk   ½ cup sugar
1 cup evaporated milk, chilled

Mix together sugar, condensed milk and soursop pulp. Pour into a covered freezer container and placed in freezer until just crystallized. Remove and beat in evaporated milk until creamy. Freeze until solid and serve. Serves 6.

Sweet Potato Pudding
~ St. Vincent ~

4 cups sweet potatoes, grated
½ cup raisins
2 cups green bananas, grated
2 teaspoons ginger, grated
2 tablespoons butter

2 cups pumpkin, grated
2 cups flour
2 cups white sugar
1 cup coconut, grated and blended with a little water in blender

1½ cups tannia, grated
1½ teaspoons cinnamon
2 teaspoons baking powder

Preheat oven to 350°F. In a large bowl, mix all ingredients together. Grease a 9 inch oven safe glass dish and dust with flour. Pour in mixture and bake at for 1½ hours. About 10 minutes before removed from oven, baste with sugar-water to keep the pudding moist. Cut into squares and serve. Serves 4.

Tablettes de Coco
~ Guadeloupe ~

2 cups freshly grated coconut
1¾ cups brown sugar

¼ teaspoon ground cinnamon
dash vanilla extract

1 cup water

In a saucepan, cook water, cinnamon and grated coconut on medium heat for 30 minutes. Lower heat and add vanilla and sugar. Simmer, stirring constantly, until you have a thick crystallized mass. Remove from heat and form the mixture into bars on a piece of confectioners' marble or a chilled oiled cookie sheet. Will keep in a closed jar in the refrigerator for 2 weeks. Makes 1 dozen.

Tamarind Balls
~ St. Kitts ~

2 cups tamarind pulp
2 cups sugar

¼ teaspoon hot red pepper, seeded and chopped
1 tablespoon salt

Remove tamarind fruit from shell and remove the seeds. Add tamarind to a pot of salted water and bring to a boil until soft. Allow to cool completely. Drain out water and add pepper. Add sugar until mixture is firm enough to form into balls. Shape mixture into balls about 1 inch in diameter and roll in additional white sugar. Wrap in waxed paper until ready to eat. Serves 2-4.

Tembleque
~ Puerto Rico ~

4 cups coconut milk
dash salt

1 teaspoon freshly ground cinnamon
½ cup cornstarch

¾ cup sugar

Moisten a 3 inch deep round dish. Dust the bottom of the dish with half of the cinnamon. Mix together 3½ cups of coconut milk, salt and sugar in a saucepan. Dissolve cornstarch in remaining milk and add gradually to saucepan. Cook on medium high and stir constantly with a wooden spoon until the liquid begins to thicken. Reduce temperature to medium. Stir until it becomes a thick custard texture. Pour into round dish and dust the remaining cinnamon on top. Refrigerate for 2 hours and serve. Serves 8-10.

Toolum
~ Trinidad ~

½ cup molasses   1 tablespoon ginger, grated   2 cups brown sugar
2 tablespoons orange zest, grated   5 cups coconut, grated

In a pan, melt brown sugar until golden brown over low heat, stirring constantly. While stirring, add molasses, ginger, orange zest and coconut. Reduce heat to very low and cook until mixture separates easily from pan. Remove from heat allow to cool. Roll mixture into cone shapes and place on a lightly oiled baking sheet. When cooled and hardened, place in an airtight container for preservation. Makes 25 sweets.

Vanilla Mousse
~ Puerto Rico ~

1 tablespoon banana, mashed   2 tablespoons fresh pineapple, puréed   dash cinnamon
3 tablespoons vanilla extract   ½ teaspoon lime juice   2 egg whites
dash salt   6 tablespoons doubled cream   2 ounces sugar

Blend pineapple and banana. Place mixture in a glass bowl and add vanilla extract, lime juice and cinnamon. In a separate bowl, beat egg whites with salt until light and frothy. Add sugar and continue to beat until stiff. Gently fold in cream. Fold the egg white mixture delicately into the fruit sauce. Spoon the mousse into frozen prepared dessert glasses. Chill for 3 hours. Garnish with fresh mint or grated orange zest. Serves 2.

Virgin Island Coconut-Pineapple Cake
~ U.S. Virgin Islands ~

1¼ cups all-purpose flour   1 (16 ounce) can pineapple chunks in natural juice, drained
¾ cup dark brown sugar   ½ cup butter, softened   2 eggs, beaten
2 teaspoons baking powder   1 teaspoon freshly ground allspice
⅔ cup unsweetened flaked coconut

Topping: confectioners' sugar   unsweetened shredded coconut

Prepare a 350°F oven and grease a loaf pan. Blend flour and sugar together well. Mix in eggs, butter, coconut, baking powder and allspice. Combine until smooth. Fold in pineapple chunks. Pour into prepared loaf pan and brush top with a little cold water. Cook for 50 minutes until risen and a skewer inserted into the center comes out clean. If cake browns too fast, cover the pan after 40 minutes and leave in pan for 10 minutes. Put on rack to cool. Turn out onto serving platter and decorate with shredded coconut and sifted confectioners' sugar. Serves 8.

Virgin Lime Pie
~ Virgin Islands ~

½ pound graham crackers, crushed
¼ teaspoon ground nutmeg
½ teaspoon cream of tartar

2 tablespoons brown sugar
½ cup fresh lime juice
1 can sweetened condensed milk

4 eggs, separated
2½ tablespoons melted butter
⅓ cup sugar

Preheat oven to 350°F. In a large bowl, mix brown sugar, melted butter, graham crackers and nutmeg. Press into an 8 inch pie form. Refrigerate. In a mixing bowl, beat the egg yolks until thick. Slowly mix in lime juice and then condensed milk. Pour mixture into the pie crust. In a small bowl, add the cream of tartar and egg whites and beat until stiff. Add sugar gradually. Beat until glossy peaks form. Spoon meringue onto pie. Bake for 20 minutes or until meringue is golden brown. Let cool. Chill for at least one hour. Serves 8.

Watermelon Sunny Mousse
~ Florida Keys ~

2 cups seeded, diced watermelon
1 envelope unflavored gelatin
2 tablespoons sugar
½ cup heavy cream

2 ripe mangoes, peeled, pitted and diced
2 tablespoons hot water
¼ teaspoon salt

3 egg whites
2 Key limes, juiced
½ teaspoon ground nutmeg

Dissolve gelatin in a small bowl with hot water. Purée mangoes in food processor for 30 seconds. Add watermelon, lime juice, sugar and gelatin and process for 30 seconds. In a mixing bowl, whip egg whites with salt until whites hold a peak. Whip the heavy cream in a separate bowl until thick and stiff. Fold the fruit mixture into the egg whites. Slowly fold in the whipped cream. Refrigerate for 3 hours. Sprinkle with nutmeg before serving.

West Indian Rock Cakes
~ St. John ~

2 cups all-purpose flour
dash salt
3 tablespoons milk
1 tablespoon grated coconut or

2 teaspoons baking powder
6 tablespoons margarine
1 tablespoon mixed candied citrus peel
1 tablespoon dried currants

½ teaspoon pumpkin pie spice
½ teaspoon brown sugar
1 egg, beaten

Prepare oven at 400°F. Grease baking pan. Sift together dry ingredients into mixing bowl. Cut in margarine until mixture resembles breadcrumbs. Lift flour to trap air in mixture. Stir in sugar and shredded coconut (or alternative). Blend in egg. Add in milk slowly, while forming dough. Using tablespoon measures, drop on to baking sheet. Bake 15-20 minutes, until golden. Serve immediately. Makes 10.

Ackee - The ackee fruit is an essential component of many popular Jamaican recipes. It has a delicate flavor and the edible portion of the ackee fruit is similar to scrambled eggs.

Agouti - A humpbacked rabbit-sized rodent that originated in South and Central America.

Allspice - Known as Jamaican pepper or pimento, it is the dried berry from a pimento tree. The berries have the appearance of peppercorns and taste like cloves, nutmeg and cinnamon. They are used either ground or whole.

Arrowroot - A powder which is white and starchy. It is used to thicken sauces and can be substituted for flour when baking.

Atemoya - A round or heart-shaped fruit with a bumpy, easily bruised green skin. The flesh is smooth and juicy with a taste similar to a virgin pina colada. Use chilled and fresh in salads, desserts and fruit drinks.

Avocado - Avocados have a delicate nutty/buttery flavor and ripen after being picked. The flesh has a smooth texture and is delicious when eaten fresh. They are used in salads, soups and garnishes.

Babaco (Mountain Papaya) - The babaco is a member of the papaya family. It is sometimes compared to the melon in flavor and texture. Eaten fresh, used for the juice or put in chutneys and desserts.

Breadfruit - A large fruit which is green in color with a pale yellow flesh resembling a potato. Breadfruit is only eaten when cooked and is used in place of potatoes, pasta or rice. It is also used as a side dish. If fresh breadfruit is not available, canned breadfruit can be used as a substitute.

Callaloo - The leaves of two separate plants: the Chinese spinach and the taro plant. They are interchangeably used, however the taro plant is more commonly used. The tubers are also used in Caribbean cooking and are known as coco or dasheen. Callaloo is similar in appearance to spinach and is similarly used.

Caribbean Red Snapper - The Caribbean waters are abundant with varieties of snapper: yellowtail, blackfin, gray, mahogany and even the dog snapper. Colors and markings vary, but the red snapper is thought to be the "caviar" of fish. The meat is soft, tasty and needs very little seasoning.

Cashew - Originally from the West Indies and South America, the cashew tree produces a fruit that is a swollen bright red stalk of flowers that yields the nut. Cashews can be expensive since they are harvested by hand.

Cassava - Originally from Brazil, it is a tuberous root also known as tapioca, yucca or Brazilian arrowroot. It can be substituted for potatoes, eddo or yams.

Chayote - A pear-shaped squash often with a prickly hair covering. Sometimes known as cho-cho, it is best when dark green. It is frequently sliced and batter fried. Young shoots can be eaten like asparagus and the leaves like greens.

Cherimoya - Used in salads, drinks, sauces, deserts and ice cream. It can also be eaten fresh and is especially good when eaten chilled and slightly soft.

Chili Peppers - Chilies are commonly used in Caribbean cooking, the most popular being the hot Scotch Bonnet. Chilies are available in different forms: crushed and bottled, as relishes, hot pepper sauces and dried chili powder.

Coconut - Coconut juice or water is the liquid located inside a fresh coconut. It is not used for cooking purposes, but is used as a mixer with rum, vodka, gin or can be consumed by itself. Coconut milk is made from the coconut flesh after having been shelled, husked and removed of the juice. The flesh is pressed to obtain the milk used in many Caribbean recipes and is also available in cans.

Cornmeal - Used in cakes, muffins, cornbread or dumplings. Cornmeal is yellow maize which is either finely or coarsely ground. Known also as maize meal or polenta, it is also used to coat food prior to frying.

Dasheen - From the same family as eddo, dasheen is peeled, boiled and served in slices with melted butter on top. The leaves of the bush are used for the base of Callaloo soup.

Dolphin - A fish (not the mammal, porpoise) also called mahi mahi: an island favorite. The fish is brilliant silver with markings of yellow-green. The filets are usually grilled, broiled, pan-fried or stuffed with seasonings.

Eddo - Native to West Africa, this tuberous root is also know as dasheen, taro or coco. It has a starch taste like potatoes.

Fig - This fruit comes in over 600 varieties and ancient Mediterranean civilizations used it as a staple in their diet. Colors of skin and flesh vary. Figs are eaten fresh or dried, and are use in dessert or for baking.

Guava - Guavas are fruit of the myrtle family tree. They can be eaten raw, however, flavor is improved by cooking. The raw fruit has a pink or white flesh with a pale yellow skin and has hundreds of hard, tiny seeds. Guavas make excellent jellies, jams and pastes. Canned guavas are also available.

Gungo Peas - Commonly used in West Indian cooking, gungo peas are also called pigeon peas. If fresh peas are not available, dried and canned can be substituted.

Jakfruit - The jakfruit is the world's largest fruit from a tree. It can weigh up to eighty pounds. It grows straight out of the trunk and branches. Upon ripening, the skin changes color from a light green to yellow or brown. The fruit is juicy and sweet with an intense aroma. It is grown in South Florida as well as the tropics.

Kingfish - Also known known as wahoo or king mackerel, it has a sharp snout with a long body. It is usually caught in deep water and next to the dolphin, is a common delicious fish in the Caribbean.

Kumquat - A fruit native to China and grown in Japan and the United States. It is the smallest citrus fruit and averages 1½ inches around. It has a thin sweet skin that is edible and a tart, juicy flesh. It is used in sauces, salads, ice cream and preserves.

Lemongrass - Grown throughout the Caribbean, lemongrass is grown to for the extraction of its essential oil. Many West Indian islands use it as a fresh herb for flavoring or as a tea in treating colds, upset stomachs or fevers.

Mammee Apple - This native fruit of the Caribbean and tropical America was part of the Native American diet upon Columbus' arrival. Mammee apples have a rind covering that is thick and bitter. The sweet orange-red pulp has quite a few large blackish seeds. They are either stewed or eaten raw.

Mango - Grown throughout the tropics and subtropics, it is native to Southeast Asia and India. There are 500 plus varieties that have different sizes, colors, shapes and flavors. The flesh is cut away from its large oval seed or pit. It is used in desserts, drinks, fruit salads and ice cream.

Mangosteen - This delicious berry is sometimes called "the Queen of tropical fruits" and is in no way related to the mango. It has a purple-brown, thick, hard shell and the waxy, white flesh is divided into segments. The shell of the mangosteen is used for the dye it makes.

Mountain Chicken - The mountain chicken, or crapaud, has been introduced into the Caribbean from Dominica. This frog has the ability to leap up to six feet. It commonly inhabits large clumps of lemon grass and feeds on snails, cockroaches, millipedes and grasshoppers. It has a delicate delicious tasting meat that is a national favorite in Dominica.

Nutmeg and Mace - Nutmeg trees were introduced to Grenada in 1843 after having been in the Caribbean for over 20 years. Today, Grenada provides almost half of the world's nutmeg and mace. The nutmeg tree will grow up to 50 feet and loves rich soil. Peculiarly, weeds never grow under it. The nutmeg flower produces a yellow, round fruit. When the fruit is ripe, it splits in half, revealing a bright red lacy membrane covering a dark brown shell. When fermented, the outer fruit makes a brandy type drink. Under the hard shell is a seed known as nutmeg. The red membrane is the mace that is used as a spice. In addition, it is a highly prized commodity for the pharmaceutical industry.

Okra - Pods of green okra are used in many soups and stews. Okra is also called bamies, ladies' fingers and gumbo.

Opossum (Manicou) - This nocturnal, shy marsupial creature carries its young in a pouch located under the stomach. Preparation of manicou in the Caribbean is varied. Dominicans smoke it, then stew it in red wine. Preferred preparation in Trinidad is to curry it.

Papaya - Derived from a woody herbaceous plant, papaya is also called pawpaw. When unripe, it is green and hard and is used in relishes and chutneys or as a vegetable. Ripened papaya is used in spicy and sweet dishes.

Parrotfish - A firm and non-oily meat. It can be fried, boiled or marinated in lime juice as an accompaniment to pigeon peas and rice.

Passion Fruit - A fruit known as maracudja or granadilla, passion fruits are wrinkly and purple when ripe. The inner buds of the passionflower allegedly symbolize the crucifixion, thus giving its name. Ice cream is made from the flesh as well as a delicious drink that is sold commercially as a syrup. Passion fruit makes a great addition to fruit salads and as a component in sauces and desserts.

Pineapple - First taken to Europe by Columbus. The pine-cone like appearance was influential in giving this tropical fruit its name. The white or yellow flesh is very juicy and can be fibrous when ripe. It is eaten fresh, used in salads, desserts or as a garnish.

Plantain - Plantains belong to the banana family and must be cooked prior to eating. They are used either green and unripe, or ripened (when the skin turns black). Their mild squash-like flavor makes them a favorite component of many West Indian dishes.

Pomegranate (Apples of Carthage) - Pomegranate trees are grown on most of the islands. The tree bears a scarlet flower and the round fruit is approximate in size to a small orange. It has a thick, smooth leathery skin that turns yellowish red when ripe. The flesh is very juicy with white seeds. Grenadine syrup is derived from Pomegranates.

Pumpkin - The Spanish speaking islands know pumpkin as calabaza. As a member of the gourd family, it is used widely in the Caribbean. It is mainly served baked, boiled or made into fritters.

Salt Codfish - Salt codfish is popular on many islands even though fresh fish is available. It must be soaked thoroughly before cooking.

Sapodilla (Nispero) - The tree this fruit grows on is the source of a white sap-chicle (used originally in chewing gum). It is grown throughout the tropics and produces a fruit that is oval to round with a russet brown, thin, rough skin. The yellow-brown flesh is slightly grainy and its flavor is sweet when fully ripe.

Shaddock - Similar to grapefruit, the juicy flesh has an intense aromatic scent. The rind is used commonly in the Caribbean for delicious crystallized sweets.

Sorrel - A small annual plant that is native to the Caribbean. Sorrel can be served raw, made into beverages both alcoholic and non-alcoholic, used to flavor jams, sauces, jellies or even ice cream. The dark red fleshy sepals that remain under the blossoms are soaked in water with different flavorings and spices. Once strained, the aromatic bright red drink, with ice added, makes a refreshing cooler.

Sour Orange - Grown widely in Spain and the Caribbean, this large orange is thought to be the ancestor to all oranges. The juice is used in marinades, marmalades and sauces.

Soursop (Guannabana) - A native to the Caribbean and tropical America. The white flesh is covered with a prickly green skin and has several black, large seeds. It is popular as a juice or as an ice cream flavor.

Star Fruit (Carambola) - The unique shape of this fruit in its cross-section gives it the name star fruit. The flavor is a combination of apple, grape and citrus. It has a waxy thin skin and a mildly sweet, soft flesh. It is mainly eaten fresh, in fruit salads or used as a garnish. Fruit that is not completely ripe is used in preserves and chutneys or to pickle.

Sugar Apple (Sweetsop) - Native to the Caribbean and tropical America, this fruit is composed of little circular knobs that form a cluster in the shape of a heart. Inside, the pulp is white and granular with a sweet, custard-like flavor. It is served raw as a dessert or can be made into a refreshing drink or ice cream. It is also used in fruit salads.

Swiss Cheese Plant (Ceriman) - Homes and offices in the Caribbean use this plant as an ornament. The fruit it produces when ripe tastes and smells like a mixture between the pineapple and the banana. The fruit is used in desserts or can be eaten right from the vine.

Tamarind - A spicy, tart pod which is long and brown. It is used in Worcestershire sauce and Angostura Bitters.

Tannia - These native Caribbean tubers are hairy and gnarled. They are boiled, baked or especially delicious parboiled then made into fritters. In some countries, tannia is mashed and mixed with coconut, eggs, sugar and spices, then baked as a pudding.

Titiri - A delicacy in Dominica, titiri are river fish and crustaceans of all kinds that have spawned by the millions. They are fully transparent and appear to be clones of each other. They appear in rivers that are still relatively pollution-free. They are caught in nets and then are quickly and thoroughly washed in sea water.

Triggerfish - The skin of a triggerfish must be immediately removed after caught to prevent the odor of its smelly skin from penetrating into the flesh. It is either deep-fried or pan-fried including the bones and is served with pigeon peas and rice.

Yams - Yams have a yellow or white flesh with a nutty flavor. They are cooked similarly to potatoes.

Yellowfin tuna - The firm meat of this fish makes it particularly delicious. Commonly sold in the form of steaks, the flesh may be dark. To retain natural juices, it should be cooked slowly with seasonings in foil.

~Index~

A

Ackee and Salt Cod 58
Acras de Morue 24
Adobo Powder 18
Antillean Carrot Cake 98
Aros Verde 50
Arpita di Pampuna 50
Arrowroot Custard 98
Arroz con Gandules 50
Arroz con Habichuelas 50
Arroz con Pollo 90
Asopao de Pollo 90
Atlantic Ginger Crayfish 58

B

Bacalaitos de San Juan 24
Balchi di Pisca (Fish Balls) 58
Banana Binja 51
Banana Breakfast Bread 12
Banana Gingersnaps 98
Banana-Rum Cake 99
Banana-Strawberry Salad 42
Banana-Vanilla Muffins 12
Banane Celeste 99
Barafie 99
Bayan Banana Peanut Soup 34
Bayan-Rum Chicken 90
Beach Lover's Red Snapper 59
Bébélé 78
Beef Pâté 78
Berehein na Forno 51
Bermuda Fish Cakes 59
Bermuda Stuffed Onions 51
Bermudan Avocado Cocktail 24
Bitterbal (Meat Croquettes) 25
Black Bean Salad 42
Bol Jul (Brule Johl) 25
Bolo di Rom 100
Breadfruit Cou Cou 51
Breadfruit Soup 34
Bridgetown Rum Cake 100
Buccaneer Crawfish with Rice 59
Buñuelos de Viento 100

C

Callaloo Soup 34
Calypso Banana-Ginger Ice Cream 101
Calypso Shrimp Créole 60
Camarones Enchilados 60
Captain Morgan's Rum Cake 101
Carambola Upside Down Delight 101
Carcó (Pickled Conch) 25
Carib Cool Papaya-Mango Sauce 18
Caribbean Best Steak 79
Caribbean Calamari Créole 60
Caribbean French Rum Toast 13
Caribbean Sea Red Snapper 61
Carnival Goat 79
Cassareep 18
Cassava Pie 91
Cayo Hueso Key Lime Salad 42

Cha-Cha-Cha-Chicken 91
Château (Chocolate Trifle) 102
Chicharrones 25
Chicken Mango Supreme 91
Christmas Cake 102
Clafoutis aux Bananas Tropicale 102
Cocada (Coconut Candy) 103
Coconut Bread 12
Coconut Cake 103
Coconut Conch 61
Coconut Cream 18
Coconut Ice Cream 103
Coconut Pudding 103
Coconut Rice and Peas 52
Coconut Rolls 13
Coconut-Shrimp Soup 35
Colombo de Poulet 92
Conch Fritters 26
Conch Salad 42
Coo-Coo 52
Cool Breeze Gazpacho 35
Coquimol 19
Crab and Shrimp Pilau 61
Crabby Cakes 62
Crabmeat Omelet 62
Crawfish Bahama-Mama 62
Creamed Garbanzo Bean Soup 35
Crema di Sorsaka (Soursop Bavarian
    Cream) 104
Créole Chicken Liver 92
Curried Chicken 92
Curried-Coconut Lobster Salad 43
Curry Cascadura 62

D

Down Island Coconut Pudding 104
Drunken Quail 93
Ducana 52
Duval Street Chilled Avocado Soup 35

E

Eddo Soup 36
Ensalada de Aguacate y Jueyes 43
Ensalada de Chayote 43
Ensalada de Pulpo 44
Essequibo Chicken 93
Extravagant Guanabana Soufflé 104

F

Famous Curried Fish with Green
    Mangoes 63
Fantasy Fest Shrimp-Mango Cocktail 26
Festival Rice Salad 44
Fish Chowder 36
Fish Fillets in Coconut 63
Fish Fritters 27
Fisherman's Special Baked Grouper 63
Fisherman's Special Grill Swordfish 64
Flan de Piña 105
Flying Fish Salad 44
Fort-de-France Blaff 64

Freeport Land Crab Soup 36
Fricassée de Langouste 64
Fricasséed Chicken 93
Fried Cracked Conch 27
Fried Fish 64
Frijoles Negros 52
Frituras de Ñame 27
Frizzle Salt Cod 65
Frozen Passion 105
Fruity Key Lime Muffins 105
Fruity Marmalade 19
Funchi 53

G

Garlic Lemon Tilapia 65
Gâteau de Patate 106
Gazpacho 37
Ginger Cake 106
Ginger Marinated Tuna 65
Giraumon Soup 37
Glorious Baked Stuffed Papaya 80
Gratin de Chayote Squash 28
Green Turtle Stew 66
Grenada Bread Pudding 106
Grilled Crocodile 80
Guava Jelly 19
Guava Sorbet 107

H

Haitian Bananes Jaunes au Gratin des
    Deux Fromages 45
Haitian Corn Fritters 28
Harinas con Jaibas 66
Hearts of Palm Salad 45
Hemingway's Great Dish 66
Holiday Ginger Broiled Tuna 67
Holiday Mango-Nut Bread 13
Hot Cross Easter Buns 107

I

Iguana Stew 80
Island Breeze Coconut and Vegetable
    Curry 53
Island Mango Sorbet 107
Island Sautéed Liver 81
Island-Style Avocado Soup 38

J

Jamaican Patties 28
Jelabi 107
Jerk Chicken 94
Johnny Cakes 14
Jug Jug 81

K

Kala 53
Karni Kabritu Stobá 81
Kerri Kerri 67
Keshi Yena 82
Kesio 108
Key Largo Key Lime Mango Shrimp 29

Key Largo Summer Drop Cookies 108
Key Lime Relish 20
Key Lime-Coconut Pie 108
Key Lime-Mango-Coconut Shrimp
    Kabobs 67
Key West Bight Meringuettes 109
Key West Garden-Style Veal Chops 82
Keys Cup 29
Keys-Style Bananas Flambé 109
Kingston Stuffed Breadfruit 54
Komkomber Stoba 82
Kumquat Treats 109

L
Langostas Enchiladas 68
Las Olas Chicken 94
Lechon Asado 83
Leg of Lamb with Mint-Guava Sauce 83
Lobster Paella 68
Lobster Patties 68
Lobster Thermidor 69
Lychee Delight 110

M
Mallory Market Mahi-Mahi 69
Mama's Best Blue Marlin Salad 45
Mama's Secret Recipe Cookies 110
Mango Cheesecake 110
Mango Chutney 20
Mango Cucumber Salad 46
Mango Glazed Lobster 70
Mango Ice Cream 111
Mango Islander Mousse 111
Mango Mojo 20
Mango Mojo Pork 83
Mango Style Grouper 70
Mango Upside-Down Delight 111
Marathon Shrimp Grapefruit Salad 46
Marzipan-Orange Meringues 111
Masala 20
Matété Crabs 70
Mazola 21
Mofongo 54
Mojo Criollo 21
Montego Bay Pineapple Chutney 21
Moros y Cristianos 54

N
Nassau Hot Crab Appetizers 29
Negril Curry Goat 84

O
Octopus Créole 71
Orange Cake 112
Orange Consommé 38
Oyster Cocktail 29
Oyster Stuffed Sea Bass 71

P
Paella de Langosta 71
Pan Bati 14

Pan de Ajo 30
Pan de Naranja 14
Papa's Favorite Potato Pie 112
Papaya and Avocado Salad 46
Papaya Ice Cream 112
Papaya Soup 38
Papaya Tropicale 47
Paradise Fowl 94
Passaat Roast Lamb 84
Passion Fruit Crème 113
Pasta a la Rasta 55
Pasteles 113
Pelau Rice 95
Pepper and Caraili Sauce 21
Pepperpot 38
Phulourie 30
Picadillo 84
Pigeon Peas and Rice 55
Pineapple Bread 14
Pineapple Pie 113
Pineapple Shrimp Cool-Me-Down
    Salad 47
Pineapple-Banana Rum Bread 15
Pirated Thyme-Mustard Sauce 22
Pisquettes 72
Point Fortin Lamb Pie 85
Poisson Grillé 72
Port Antonio Jerk Swordfish Kabobs 72
Port au Prince Lambi Créole 73
Port of Spain Mango-Curried Shrimp 73
Port Royal Bammie 15
Puerto Plata Sweet Corn Bread 16

Q
Quesillo (Crème Caramel) 114

R
Rabbit Fricassée 85
Ragoût de Boeuf 85
Rasta Salad 47
Red Snapper a la Créole 73
Reggae Curried Chicken 95
Riz et Pois Colles 55
Roasted Wild Pig with Red Wine Sauce 86
Ropa Vieja 86
Roti 16
Rum and Raisin Fudge 114
Rum Banana Brulée 114
Rum Raisin Pigeon 95

S
Saint Lucian Grapefruit-Avocado Salad 47
Saltfish and Ducana 74
Saltfish Pie 74
San Juan's Piononos con Plantanos 86
Santo Domingo Red Snapper Fricassée 74
Saté 87
Savory Palomilla Steak 87
Seafood a la Gros 75
Shipwreck Grouper with Fiery
    Eggplant Sauce 75

Sofrito 22
Sopa de Gandules 39
Sopa de Pollo 39
Sorrel Jam 22
Soursop Ice Cream 114
Souskai d' Avocats 30
Southernmost Point Conch Chowder 39
St. George Garlic Pork 87
St. John Fry Fish 75
St. John Plantain Grouper 76
St. John's Coconut Mussels 30
St. Thomas Curried Scallops 76
Stamp and Go (Fish Fritters) 31
Star Fruit Wake-Me-Ups 16
Stone Crab Salad 48
Stuffed Breadfruit 31
Stuffed Crab Backs 31
Sunny Pumpkin Soup 40
Sunshine Citrus Salad 48
Sweet Pork Tenderloin 87
Sweet Potato and Tomato Soup 40
Sweet Potato Pudding 115

T
Tablettes de Coco 115
Taino Seafood Stew 40
Tamarind Balls 115
Tannia Fritters 32
Tembleque 115
Titiri Ackra 32
Toolum 116
Tortilla Clásica Española 56
Tostones 32
Treasured Chicken 96
Trinidad Pilau 96
Trinidad Style Curried Lamb 88

V
Vanilla Mousse 116
Veal Chops a la Jardinera 88
Virgin Eggplant 56
Virgin Island Coconut-Pineapple
    Cake 116
Virgin Kallaloo 88
Virgin Lime Pie 117
Virgin Lobster Salad 48
Virgin Lobster Stew 32
Virgin Seasoning 22

W
Watermelon Sunny Mousse 117
West Indian Rock Cakes 117

Y
Yam Balls 56
Yellowfin Tuna in Vanilla-Rum Flambé 76

ORDER ONLINE - www.bluewaterislands.com
For Antique Maps visit - www.classicmapart.com

If you would like calendars or our books, please make a copy of this order form. Send check or money order to our address below. If you would like to place an order by credit card, you may call us at 954-680-1771. Minimum orders for credit cards, $25.00. Please order early because quantities are limited.

	PRICE	QUANITY	TOTAL
~CALENDARS~			
Key West Calendar (12x12 inches with over 40 pictures)	$9.95	_____	_____
~BOOKS~			
Florida Keys/Key West (32 Pages, over 100 pictures)	$5.95	_____	_____
(Text in English, French, Spanish and German, 7x10 inches)			
Key West/Florida Keys (48 Pages)	$8.95	_____	_____
(Coffee Table Book with over 60 pictures)			
Florida Book (80 Pages, over 145 pictures)	$9.95	_____	_____
(Text in English, French, Spanish and German, 8x11 inches)			
American Lighthouses (32 Pages, over 120 pictures)	$5.95	_____	_____
(7x10 inches with all color pictures)			
Don't Stop The Party (Over 120 pages)	$9.95	_____	_____
(A complete guide to Tropical Drink Recipes from the Florida Keys)			
Don't Stop The Cook (Over 120 pages)	$9.95	_____	_____
(A complete guide to Caribbean Food Recipes)			
~SCREENSAVERS~			
American Lighthouses (70 pictures, wallpaper and sound)	$12.95	_____	_____
(For Windows™ 95, 98, Me, 2000, XP, NT)			
Key West & The Florida Keys (70 pictures, wallpaper and sound)	$12.95	_____	_____
(For Windows™ 95, 98, Me, 2000, XP, NT)			
~STATIONERY~			
Florida Keys Memo Pad (5½x8 inches, 50 pages with 6 photos)	$3.95	_____	_____
Key West Memo Pad (5½x8 inches, 50 pages with 6 photos)	$3.95	_____	_____
Florida Keys Magnetic Notepad (4x9 inches, 50 pages)	$3.95	_____	_____
(with 9 photos, magnetic strip on backside)			
Key West Magnetic Notepad (4x9 inches, 50 pages)	$3.95	_____	_____
(with 9 photos, magnetic strip on backside)			
Florida Keys Writing Journal (6x8¼ inches, 80 ruled pages)	$7.95	_____	_____
Key West Writing Journal (6x8¼ inches, 80 ruled pages)	$7.95	_____	_____
~PLAYING CARDS~			
Florida Keys (54 card deck, different pictures on each card)	$5.00	_____	_____
Caribbean (54 card deck, different pictures on each card)	$5.00	_____	_____
American Lighthouses (54 card deck, different pictures on each card)	$5.00	_____	_____

SHIPPING CHARGES

$ 0.00 - $ 9.99 — $ 4.50	Overseas orders of
$10.00 - $19.99 — $ 5.50	$50.00 or less add
$20.00 - $35.00 — $ 7.00	$13.00 to the
$35.01 - $50.00 — $ 9.00	shipping
$50.01 - $75.00 — $11.00	charge prices.
over $75.00 — $13.00	

Prices subject to change.
SHIPPING: Most shipping is handled by UPS or the Post Office. Please list street address. All orders are not necessarily shipped together. All items are satisfaction guaranteed or your money will be promptly refunded if returned in good condition within 30 days.

Total All Items _____

FL Residents add
6% Sales Tax _____

Shipping Charges _____

Total Due _____

Visa / Mastercard

_____ _____ _____
Card Number   Exp. Date   Signature

Please make sure that your billing address of the credit card is the same as your shipping address!

PRINT NAME: _____

STREET ADDRESS: _____

_____

CITY: _____

STATE: _____ ZIP: _____ PHONE: _____

We also accept Checks or Money Orders payable to:
Pro Publishing, Inc.
P.O. Box 266601
Weston, FL 33326
954-680-1771